Resilience, Grace and the Art o
uplifting sharing of one youn
and rise above the traumas that had affected her in childhood by opening up to life and new possibilities of perceiving and understanding herself and life.

She made the shift from victim to victor, enlightening the reader to access the Power of Nature as ally and healer, awakening us to our own innate resilience.

Her journey took her around the world for several decades, where she immersed herself in many different cultures, explored different religions and philosophies of life, looking to find matching reflections of the deeper hidden truths in life that she had always felt connected to that she witnessed in Nature.

Luannah offers deep insights and tools of perception in how we can recreate ourselves and restore harmony and balance after trauma. This book has the power & potential to change lives in beautiful and enriching ways.

"*Luannah Victoria Arana* has penned a Heroine's Journey of adventures, trauma and profound healing. May all find this book deeply inspiring in their personal journey to wholeness."
-Mare Cromwell, Author *The Great Mother Bible & Messages From Mother Earth*

"*Resilience Grace and the Art of Showing Up* is a courageous memoir and a source of hope that a wonderous life is possible on the other side of trauma and pain. It is a beautiful tale of overcoming trauma and stepping into an empowered version of yourself. Even in her darkest moment Luannah finds Grace everywhere. Seekers everywhere will relate and recognize themselves in Luannah and her faith, her sensitivity, her intuition and in her practices for healing and wholeness. The forgiveness she displays is heartening. Even in the midst of some really hard knocks, she beachcombs for treasures, and finds them every time. Gratitude fills her book. Luannah didn't just survive, she went on to thrive and pay it forward in her Healing Centre." -Maryse Cardin, Author *Speaking to Yourself with Love: Transform Your Self Talk*

"Luannah is an inspiring person, as is her story of the many layers of learning, healing and transformation she has experienced that she shares here. *Resilience, Grace and the Art of Showing Up* is a powerful message of encouragement to those who are on a path of personal growth." -Mahmud Nestman, Counsellor M.Ed, RCC,HT

"Resilience Grace and the Art of Showing Up is an expression of faith, fortitude and forgiveness. Luannah shares her experiences and adventures in life overcoming trauma. An honest and at times heart wrenching depiction of her tenacity and courage to reach the life lessons to become her true self. A truly gifted human has evolved who now enriches and empowers others through her energy and resurgence." -Andrea Davis, Author *Survival Was Only The Beginning*

"This is a compelling Manuscript, full of emotional and physical abuse that has been overcome by a young woman's fortitude and willingness to learn from her experience. The author's adventures were amazing and powerful; readers will deeply admire her spirited attempts to come to an understanding about what—and why –things were happening to her. And they will root for her to overcome (which she did)." -Bill Worth, Editor

RESILIENCE, GRACE AND THE ART OF SHOWING UP

*A Spiritual Journey of
Empowerment Against All Odds*

Luannah Victoria Arana

Paperback ISBN: 978-1-64184-211-2

Ebook ISBN: 978-1-64184-212-9

Published by JETLAUNCH.

Dedication

To my loving husband Juan Carlos Arana,
without your loving support this book
may have not come to completion,
I love you so much and am so grateful you are in my life.
To my beautiful son, Isaac Nathanial, you are such a
shining and bright light in my heart and life,
filling me with so much joy and love.
You teach me so much every day.
To my parents, who gave me life, who have grown and
healed with me, and with whom I now share so much love.

I also dedicate this book in loving memory
to Carole Groddeck otherwise known as Hathor,
my Mentor and Teacher,
to Brigitte and Peter Forster who were both loving
guides and friends in some of my darkest hours,
without them I may not have made it through.

Also to Gillian Murshall, a bright soul that I loved
and cared for dearly who left us too soon to suicide,
this loss propelled me to complete this book
sooner than later,
with the hope it can be a light of inspiration for those
struggling in pain and confusion as she did.

CONTENTS

INTRODUCTION

"The gift that lies waiting for us is growth, is change.
It's the possibility that something good can come from pain.
And when the crisis hits,
and our world comes tumbling down,
when we are afraid,
will we have the strength and the wisdom
to embrace the gift that is there,
and welcome it with open arms?"
– From *Being Erica*

This book shares my journey of self-discovery through the many landscapes of painful experiences and challenges I have encountered in my life and how I overcame the effects of abuse and trauma through my connection with Nature. I thankfully found my way back home to myself, to my heart and to my original joy of living. After many years of having so many people who I shared my journey with tell me I should write a book, here it is.

My life is a testament to, and a reflection of, the power we all have to rise above adversity and how we can claim our power to overcome what holds us back, how we can grow beyond trauma patterns that keep us repeating beliefs and behaviours that limit our capacity for healing and authentic self-expression.

My book is also an ode to nature, revealing how connecting to nature as a way to self-reflect, to nourish and activate our innate creativity and resilience teaches and nourishes us in times of adversity and challenge. Nature's resilience is an active force in all of us that grants us the capacity to meet challenges with confidence and affirmative action. Some confuse resilience with perseverance, where we just 'push through' with force and strength. When we only push through without really leaning in and growing our understanding and awareness through the challenges we are actually building stress in the body by burying over the emotions and pain that get ignored by only pushing through.

Though there is an element in resilience that exhibits perseverance, as I have come to understand, resilience is more about our capacity to creatively utilize challenges and adversity to our benefit. Where we become more than we were, that we could not have otherwise become, because of the challenges, pains etc. that we encounter in life. Nature reveals to us that creative response in how it adapts and uses otherwise interrupting forces and influences for its support and growth. Nothing can stop Nature from growing and becoming. Like a tree I saw in Berlin that inspired this insight in me that grew its trunk around a wire fence flourishing beautifully in spite of the fences presence.

Resilience, I have learned, is about creativity, courage and commitment to grow no matter what. The willingness to use all that comes our way to grow and evolve us. Nature is the greatest teacher and example of this capacity that is an innate capacity in us as well. Nature has been my ultimate inspiration and teacher in knowing myself and healing from trauma.

This book is also about recognizing how we are all connected, how we are in the same boat together, struggling with the very same things every day that no one talks about.

Here in this Introduction I am going to share some thoughts and observations that have the potential to open your mind and heart to new possibilities of living and perceiving life that can bring a new sense of empowerment, liberation and freedom. I share these as a way to invite you into my inner world and to prepare you for the story you are about to read so you can frame it in a way that makes sense and that what is shared can inspire you to know yourself and the magic and beauty that awaits every one of us when we show up to meet and heal ourselves.

There are many common threads that connect us all, all of Humanity, all of Nature. One of these threads is that we all experience adversarial forces. We encounter intense circumstances that challenge us to find and create new ways to survive and hopefully, also thrive.

We also all experience pain, confusion, doubt, loss, suffering, fear, and moments of depression in the span of our life, where we ask, and sometimes cry out in anguish, "Why? Why me? Why is this happening? Why can't I figure this out? Why, Why, Why?" We feel forsaken by ourselves, God/Love, the whole Universe.

This leads us to another common experience we all share ... the fear, confusion and discomfort of "not knowing". To admit we do not know brings us into feeling vulnerable in life, a feeling we most often do our best to avoid and ignore. Because of this fear, we develop a need to conclude everything we are feeling and experiencing into a singularity. Creating a singular definition enables us to convince ourselves that we know what we think we know. We then no longer question our way of perceiving.

This 'knowing', then becomes the foundation of our beliefs and identity through which we filter everything.

This causes us to interpret all our life experiences and the people we encounter in an extremely dualistic way. Our actions and reactions then become solely based upon these biased belief systems that we have both grown up, with influenced by family and society, as well as those we cultivated through life experiences. There is no room for anything outside of our worldview. No room to learn and grow. No room to Change.

We cling to what we believe we know so strongly, as a way to feel safe in the world, that we become inflexible to anything outside our comfort zone. This results in us feeling stuck and caught in such narrowness that it suffocates our capacity to grow and change. But Nature is all about change. Change is the only constant we can count on. So when we are afraid of change we are going against the natural flow and rhythms of life itself. Is it any wonder we feel depressed and uninspired? If we were a plant and refused to be affected by the ever shifting forces of Nature that give us life, we would die quite quickly. Why do we block the natural flow? Why does the 'unnatural' come to feel so natural to us? Safety is why.

Every one of our basic primal needs is to feel safe. That is the highest priority to our nervous system. Every room we walk into, every person we meet, every new situation, in the depth of our biology we are asking 'am I safe? am I safe? am I safe?' This need for safety has us construct beliefs and interpretations that act as a barrier in us to create a sense of safety. Our beliefs become our fortress of safety. For the most part they serve us well, we need beliefs to define and navigate the world, but when we have been traumatized we become even more narrow in our perceptions and leaving our comfort zone feels absolutely threatening, so we lock ourselves in deeper and deeper in our beliefs, afraid to let go of our story that it could endanger us opening and letting ourselves be vulnerable. In this state singular truths feel like our saving Grace, *this is good, this is bad, this is right, this is wrong, I like, I don't like.* We lose the capacity to think and observe the more subtle and complex nature of life and ourselves, which requires an expanded mind to see and comprehend the complexity of our life and experiences with greater clarity and accuracy.

In my experience and in witnessing the lives around me, I see this as a main cause to our internal suffering. In reality, no truth is singular, trying to reduce everything to a single cause or single truth is what spins us in circles. It is impossible. Truth is always layered and often with many contrary truths that can co-exist simultaneously that are equally valid and true. When I attempt to reduce and conclude an experience, a person or result to a singular truth or interpretation I omit nuances and contexts that are vitally important to cultivating understanding of the world around me and of my experiences, particularly the painful ones. Once we get ensnared in our inner dogmas, which ultimately limit possibility versus embracing and opening to it, it then tends to send us into deeper chaos and confusion.

Through my life experiences I have learned that to truly see and gain knowledge so that I can heal I need to expand my view, not contract and reduce it. I need to be inclusive, allowing everything, every feeling, every thought, every experience its place and purpose.

Our limbic and nervous system, however, is hardwired to protect us when we have experienced trauma. We reduce and exclude in order to simplify to survive. So, to go against that survival program can be really challenging. Even though our brains are also hardwired to adapt and change as well, once the trauma response is activated we can easily get locked in to habits and beliefs created to keep us safe that do not serve our greater evolution of self and soul.

Opening to something new, coupled with the experience of not knowing are two of the most difficult experiences to navigate in life, even more so when something traumatic has taken place. It is generally hard for us to admit we don't know something. We are compelled to believe and feel this incessant need to know and understand everything immediately. If we don't, we suffer. We judge ourselves for not knowing. We judge life for being so "hard and cruel," for not making sense. We feel lost, alone, confused, and angry.

But what if there is another way of observing and perceiving available to us? What if not knowing was something to actually celebrate and embrace? What if it was something to be excited about because it means we have the opportunity to go beyond what we currently know, to discover something new that can enrich our lives and relationships? What if our perception shifted in that direction and made it okay to temporarily not know? What if we can feel good about life and ourselves that something happened to shake our perceptions, to make us uncertain, because it opens us to new possibilities? What if?

These are the questions that arose in me from the traumas I experienced that propelled me to dive deep into my story in order to heal it, where I had to question my beliefs and uncover the ones that I had created to 'protect myself', that were actually sabotaging my healing and growth.

Hawaiian teachings is one branch of wisdom that brought a lot of goodness to my life and helped increase my capacity to shift my perceptions from feeling like a victim to being empowered and helped me open to new possibilities. I will share a little bit here.

In Hawaiian teachings, as I was taught, the principle of Kala means I am free. When I am free, there are no limits to prevent me from healing and creating the life of my dreams. It opens the world of possibilities. With Kala I understand that the world is how I perceive it, and that the world will always reflect my perceptions back to me. With Kala it is understood that all systems and beliefs are actually arbitrary. They are merely formed and created by our mind making the best attempt to define reality, to define the mystery and ineffable nature of ourselves and life. It reveals that just because we choose to believe what we believe does not mean it is true or in alignment with Universal Laws and what is true.

What is the measure of truth? How do we measure if something is true? Most of us base our interpretations of truth on strong feelings and emotions. But how do we discern whether it is our wound or an inherited negative belief system activating our emotions, then directing our thoughts and perceptions, versus, our perceptions coming from clarity of presence in the moment, knowledge and insight?

My time in Hawaii helped me to learn and discern the difference with greater effectivity. The teachings I learned in Hawaii reflected so many wisdoms and truths, that I had already discovered and explored in Nature, into greater clarity and integration for me. The profound simplicity and depth of the life teachings they offer is life changing. It brought order to my scattered mind and emotions, and integration where my traumas had left me fragmented. One cannot remain a victim living by the principles they share, and I was looking to get out of the victim beliefs that still had a hold on me.

One of the other Hawaiian Principles that helped me become congruent within myself and the world is Pono. In Hawaii I was taught that every word and every wisdom has seven levels of depth and meaning. Some of the meanings of Pono are Truth, Genuineness and Honesty. The Principle Pono is a navigational awareness and tool that also translates as, 'effectiveness is the measure of truth', meaning that if the belief or action we are undertaking works in harmony with the laws of nature and life to sustain and uphold ourselves and life, to sustain good, and it helps us to do and be better, then it's considered true and effective. We come to see that our beliefs either evolve and lift us or they corrode and devolve us away from our higher nature.

As mentioned before, though arbitrary in nature, our beliefs and labels do serve a certain function that enables us to create definition in our lives. The beliefs we create and align with give us a sense of safety. Yet, when we become stuck in those beliefs and labels, when we create our own personal dogmas from them that then limit other possibilities from touching and affecting us in a way that can evolve us to new levels of understanding and wisdom, then there is a serious problem.

One of the hardest things to do when recovering from Post-Traumatic Stress Disorder is allowing ourselves to be vulnerable and open to a new way of perceiving and believing. It's hard because our personal stories and dogmas we created to cope and survive do keep us safe. We crave control of ourselves and our environment to feel safe. Our beliefs give us that safety. Right, wrong, true or indifferent, they keep us safe, which is why we rarely question them. Hence the more traumatized we are, the less open we are to change. But being open to change and new thought is the only thing that can save us from our own self-made walls that may protect us in some ways, but they also block and keep the good stuff out, like love, fun, intimacy and healing.

In my years of overcoming PTSD, I struggled a lot to open myself beyond my story. My mind had become quite focused on the traumas, rigid and closed in many ways, and if anyone challenged, without kindness, the beliefs that kept me safe, I would shut down towards them and isolate myself more from the world.

By the time I arrived to Hawaii in 2010 I had already healed, expanded and opened myself immensely, but I still got stuck sometimes and pulled into traumatic loops. Less often albeit, but it still happened. The teachings and healings I received in Hawaii helped me that next step I needed to go to restore my heart and trust in life fully. I was reborn.

Kala- I am free, there are no limits, all systems and beliefs are arbitrary… this really liberated me from debilitating beliefs that didn't serve me anymore. I explored and observed the difference between beliefs I inherited from family and society and the one's I created from my own experiences, what beliefs served me and what one's didn't. Realizing I can choose which beliefs heal and evolve me versus those that don't. I can choose beliefs that include diversity and change or not. It's up to me what I choose in every moment.

When we have trauma we have so many filters that dilute life and our own vitality. I know what it takes to stretch beyond the comfort zone to trust to let life in its fullness after abuse and trauma. It is not an easy journey, but it is possible with love and kindness towards ourselves, which opens us to heal.

It's incredibly freeing to recognize the arbitrary nature of the beliefs and thoughts we choose to create and feed. It's also a tricky thought process to wrap our mind around. Since we can find validation for any thought and belief we choose, good or bad how do we discern what is right action or wrong action? We can't base it on belief alone. We need something like an inner compass to guide us. A compass that shows us what is effective in affirming life, enabling us to love and care for ourselves and each other, a compass that brings us into harmony with the universal laws that govern all creation. That can bring us in alignment with our higher nature which is our connection to the God force in us and in all life. How can we find that inner compass? When I watch bugs and animals in nature they seem to have an inner compass that always leads them exactly where they need to be to attain the nourishment and environment that supports them to grow and thrive. All of Nature is well equipped, then so must we be. We need to look and dig deep into ourselves to find it. What if I open myself to the possibility that I must have the same kind of inner guidance system as nature that simply got blocked somehow, that I can connect to in times of pain and confusion?

Pause for a moment while reading this if you will, to explore and feel the possible freeing impact of that way of perceiving and navigating, if you knew beyond a doubt that you are wired to know what you need and where to go for it. That all you have to do is look for and activate that innate inner compass. What would it open in you to realize this and that there are other possibilities of perception that are equally valid as your current ones, that could even possibly expand and evolve you beyond where you currently are in your inner and outer worlds? Really feel in to it. Can you feel the simplicity and freedom it offers? Can you feel the space it creates for something new to come in and be inspired by? Like a fresh breeze. Can you feel the tension release in your body? Take a deep breath.

If all systems and beliefs are arbitrary, are a matter of choice, and are our creation, what then blocks us from choosing a new, more life-affirming definition or path? What stops us from choosing a path that increases our capacity to love? What inhibits us from questioning ourselves and our beliefs that are feeding our suffering, anger and pain? I discovered that our innate inner compass will always direct us towards what is good and wholesome to support us to thrive when it is fully activated and intact, we just need to clear the interference and tune in.

What stops so many of us from choosing a path that is inclusive of diversity and welcomes change? What if we choose a way of perceiving that is not based on a reductionist point of view but, rather an expansive and inclusive one that observes and validates the complexity and subtle nuances that allows two contrary truths to co-exist at the same time, as they often do, with equal validity.

What happens when we can allow the paradox of living to be what it is? Where we can drop the battle of who's right and who's wrong based on our beliefs and then create space to explore, learn and understand new ways of being, feeling and perceiving, rather than fighting and competing all the time?

Exploring these questions and earnestly seeking the answers has been and is at the core of my life journey. When I was a little girl I remember always asking why people fought, it didn't make sense to me at all. My life has brought me many teachings and insights since then. I now understand what lies at the core of conflict; it is our pain and trauma. It is the defensive and protective mechanisms we create to feel safe that create so many misunderstandings in our relationships, both with ourselves and each other.

In all my years of studying myself, psychology, science, human nature and spirituality, Hawaiian teachings brought it all together for me and revealed to me, to my surprise, how I had already been governing my life with the same insight and understanding that they share. I was already living the same principles without knowing it my whole life. The teachings of Nature are indeed universal!

What I have come to understand from Nature is that it will grow weeds and orchids equally. In the same way our focus and attention will feed, grow and validate our reality through our beliefs and perceptions. The God force in us, will amplify and grow whatever thoughts and beliefs we repeat and feed. This is the principle of Makia-Focus. Where my attention goes, energy flows and that is the reality that grows.

We live in a world of vibrational energy with Laws of Resonance, Attraction and Magnetism that take part in our daily lives and creations. To understand this gives us more creative control in directing our life. This is where my connection to Nature served me so well. Though I had never been to Hawaii before, I witnessed these same principles in Nature as a young girl, and it is these insights that brought me through so much pain and trauma that you will read about in this book.

So when in my late thirties, when I was just coming out of a lot of processing and rebuilding myself, I discovered Hawaii and started learning with my teachers there, you can imagine, I felt instantly at home. I felt completely found and met in every way. It is effortless for me to be me there.

As I have come to see it, due to our collective forgetting that we are a part of nature and that we are subject to the same rules and laws, we have basically created the mess we are in, both personally and globally. When we reconnect to the awareness that we are nature, and use that understanding to guide us, hope and new possibilities are born, there is new direction and we can begin to co-create our lives with more harmony love, creativity and intention.

It is important to understand that for any change or metamorphosis to take place in Nature, there has to be an interruption or deviation from the original patterns that held it in its original form. Like the caterpillar. In the in-between state from being a caterpillar to becoming a butterfly, there is absolute chaos happening in the biology. Everything changes. The cells that once governed the systemic order lose their power in order to be transformed into a new order and function. I went through this transformative process many times in my life where absolutely everything fell apart and I was in the recreative process of chaos for quite some time before coming out the other end, renewed and more whole.

Every time we experience "adversarial forces" and experiences that challenge our perception and view of ourselves and life, it is an opportunity to explore and create ourselves anew. For me, what is absolutely certain, is that conflict and experiencing adversarial forces has been an essential key to my evolution, and is a key to all our evolution that we continually overlook and miss because we focus on the negative impact and therefore we focus on the battle of life. As much pain and trauma as I have experienced, what got me through was looking for the learning each time. What could I learn about myself and how to do, be and think differently, that will make me more whole and stronger, that I wouldn't learn otherwise without whatever conflict or abuse I encountered. That way of perceiving worked to evolve me my whole life and still does.

What if you were to choose to explore and navigate all life challenges with that understanding and perception? How might your life change for the better? What if you choose to look to nature for what you need? What if you see how the intelligence, patterns and chaos of nature are a reflection of you? What if you embrace not knowing with curiosity and joy rather than fearing it?

When did not knowing become something to fear in first place? To understand our fear it is useful to reflect beyond our current time to find the roots.

Reflecting on history, I see how the belief systems we have inherited from generations past have imprinted us with the feeling that not knowing is to be feared like death.

We are afraid to admit we don't know something, lest we be laughed at or perceived as inadequate. This was an important observation for me in overcoming my own limitations and fears. I saw how I blocked new information that had the potential to transform my life because I was afraid to acknowledge I didn't know. To be receptive to new information I have to open myself, which means I have to be vulnerable, and I have to acknowledge that maybe my way of being up until then wasn't the most effective way to navigate. We also use the statement *"I Know"* as a great deflector that blocks the new from touching us.

I am not the only one. I witness it repeatedly with my clients and people I meet all the time. Our sense of value has been greatly based on what we can declare we know. Through this obsession of mind knowledge as a way to show self-value and worth in the world -- to feel powerful and better than others -- we have disconnected with a much more innate and important knowledge that waits for every human being to connect to... the knowledge of nature and our intricate connectedness to all things and each other and the impact our beliefs and thoughts have on ourselves, each other and our environment. Even Quantum physics validates this fact.

This vibrational force of wisdom and intelligence is the core of everything in existence. That has never changed and will never change. It is a vibrational Truth, if you will, that exists, whether I exist or not to witness and define it. This Truth has been experienced, written about, and expressed since the beginning of humanity, in every culture and tradition. The awareness of these vibrational truths and wisdoms were at the beginning and core of every religion and faith.

A part of our healing is rewiring ourselves to remember and regain our innate relationship to this vibrational truth in Nature, our true nature. To awaken our inner compass. To connect to those forces of Nature within us, that we all have access to when we choose to, that have the power to catalyze shifts in our awareness that then bring about the lasting transformation and healing we all long for to live a more fulfilling and happy existence.

The ultimate power of Nature is it's capacity to transmute, transform and refine in all living beings and things. It is also our ultimate power. We often fear that power though because real transformation can be a scary process where we have to temporarily let go of all the beliefs and stories that protect us in order to create a new 'order' within.

Unfortunately, because of our fears of change, the battle of who knows more, who can gain more power and who has the best definition and interpretation of the 'truth' of this vibrational force we call God became, and still is, more important than the connection to 'God' itself.

Getting confused with the belief of 'needing to know' as a way to feel powerful, important and that we belong, is where I see we, as a collective humanity, disconnected and lost sight of the unity of all life and energy. This is where we became disconnected from seeing and knowing that every living being under the sun already does belong. We all belong. We all contribute to the whole, we don't have to do or be anything special to belong. Due to that disconnect we have lost our capacity to connect to that energy to find our unique place and purpose in life. This belief also rippled down to how we engage each other and all our relationships. The prime directive for living and succeeding became power instead of connection. Which translates as competition rather than collaboration. If you look at all the issues we have in the world, personally and globally, the battle for power is at the core.

When that disconnection from Nature occurred, knowledge of the mind, based on arbitrary interpretations and definitions of the time, were given more power and authority than the innate presence of wisdom in everyone and every living thing and being. This separation has led to much harm and abuse in our world and in our relationships. Humanity and Nature has been suffering because of so much misinformation and misperceptions that have numbed us out of our interconnectedness.

However, in spite of anything that has happened to you in life and in your life, or anyone else, we all have within us the ability to connect to the inner resilience in nature within us to use the adversarial forces, the pain etc., in our life, to our benefit. We can leverage painful experiences toward healing, joy and empowerment.

All ancient cultures knew that as a fact, beyond a doubt, including Ancient Hawaiian's. How did they know that? Who told or showed them that you might ask?

Nature did.

> "The truest reflection of our true Nature is Nature."
> - Thoreau

Do you know you are loved? Do you know that you matter? Do you know that you are enough?

Nature is the reflection of just how much you are loved. There is nothing in the natural world that does not belong and is not connected to that powerful and resilient life force that nourishes and supports everything you see around you, including you to live. This flow of Love/Life Force is the one constant in life we can access and count on. It is the one constant that nourished me and guided me through my life to become who I am today; healed, whole and thriving against all odds like the flowers on the cover of this book.

We are all an aspect and expression of nature. We are all made of the same elements, just configured differently. So, why would you or anyone be exempt from that Love and support?

When we look to Nature and watch the rhythms and cycles, we see the unequivocal evidence of this incredible innate resilience that allows and causes life to persist, to bloom and grow, regardless of challenges and "adversarial" forces. I call that the force of Love.

A tree will grow through and around a fence. A blade of grass will push itself through a crack in the cement sidewalk, relentlessly determined to birth itself through to the light of day. After forest fires, trees grow that could not have grown without the fire activating the seeds. There are countless examples of this unlimited power of nature pushing through, determined to live and be what it is meant to be, no matter what. Nature is always creating and recreating itself in its full glory and beauty. We are designed to be supported, resilient and thrive in the same way.

Nature saved my life. Literally. I would not be here today to write this book if not for my connection to Nature.

In Nature I found reflections of life and of myself that helped me make sense of it all, and ultimately heal my traumas. Nature helped me find my way back to my stolen and lost innocence. Being in Nature helped me connect to and understand that ineffable, invisible force we call God.

From a very early age, and throughout my entire life, Nature has been my Bible. My refuge. My source of Love, deep insight, and regeneration.

As a great teacher, Mikael Omraam Ivanov, once said, "*The first Bible was never written. It exists in Nature as Nature. Whenever someone tries to convince me of a theory or philosophy, I check in nature if I cannot find an equal reflection of whatever is being claimed, I dismiss it immediately!*"

When I read that in a book of his in my early twenties, I felt so affirmed. I hadn't fully consciously grasped the profoundness of Nature's effect on me until my twenties. I always just knew that I felt more "me" in Nature. I felt alive in Nature. I felt revitalized and lovingly held by the oceans and lakes, by the earth, trees, and mountains.

It's as if there is a non- verbal language that passes between our soul and Nature, but we have to still ourselves enough to consciously tune in and receive the "download" of love that Nature has for every one of us when we take the time to tune in. When I fully understood this I intentionally went to Nature more, particularly when I was distressed.

You may have also been supported by those loving invisible forces, whispering to your heart and soul, nourishing and guiding you to keep going without really realizing it.

How do you know if the trees, oceans, and Earth are supporting you? If you feel more yourself when you are in Nature. If going for a walk in Nature energizes you, inspires you to paint, dance, or write poetry then you are connecting and being nourished by the love of Nature. Imagine if you start intentionally engaging Nature, how deep those feelings may take you.

St Francis of Assisi, who inspired my life greatly in my late twenties and still does, also connected to Nature and saw God in all life, and saw nature as a direct path to connect to God.

As I have been taught, the Native Hawaiian understanding of God is that there is no word that can be named that is sufficient. I completely agree. In Hawaiian teachings God is a verb, not a noun. God is known as the action force in all creation. It is the force that is always creating, transforming, supporting, growing, inspiring, and encouraging life, Nature, us, to reach our fullest expression. This "God" Force is constantly flowing and insists on growing and becoming more of itself, fulfilling its original design and blueprint to manifest every expression that is true to its real nature and purpose, which is Aloha, Love.

Ancient Mystery School teachings did not call God a creator, as most religions and some traditions do either; they called that force *The Prime Mover.* That is another reflection that what we call God is a creative and active force in motion.

You are also a creative and active force in motion. That God force is beating your heart and moving through you every moment of your existence. It is the force that ignites inspiration, love and hope. Feel it. Know it. You are designed and equipped to grow and be uniquely you.

Since we are Nature, separate in no way other than by our minds, perceptions, and beliefs, we are subject to its Laws and Rules. These include The Law of Resonance, The Laws of Magnetism and Attraction, as well as the Laws of Life and Death and Rebirth.

Recognizing and understanding this was and is so vital to my healing and evolution. It helps me realize that the choices I make activate a response in the world around me. Everything is energy. Again, Quantum Physics shows us that observation instantly changes what is being observed by the observer.

Instead of being successful creating our misery and suffering through our focus and attention on the "bad" in life, why not choose to be successful creating the opposite, using and magnifying the good in others and life to create a happier and more fulfilling life. We are the chooser in every moment. That choice needs to be made every moment. Knowing I have that choice gave me freedom from everything that had once pinned me down in darkness and depression. Knowing that all of Nature is on my side and there to support and inspire me helped me create the changes in belief and perception I needed to in order to heal.

What if you were to choose to observe life differently, in a way that upholds the good in you and your life? How might that affect positive change? These were some questions I asked myself when I would find myself in a funk. I have learned that we have the power and ability to grow and create our lives to fulfill our deepest soul longings and dreams when we direct our attention and focus wholeheartedly towards bettering ourselves and Love.

In my life I have experienced validation after validation of this truth. The hard and painful things I have gone through, the abuses I have endured -- yet by some magical force, I have come through -- healed and restored in my heart.

That magical force is the combination of Nature and me. My constant choice to connect to that love, to keep learning, keep growing, pushing through it all like that blade of grass is what brought me to the beautiful and fulfilling life I am living today.

Nature has the Power to heal us when we connect. The thing is, that unlike trees and plants and animals in the natural world, because we have consciousness and the facility of thinking, we need to direct our attention and focus to this resilient life force, Love, in order to set it in motion at times of struggle and illness, to help us learn and grow. There are actions we need to take to activate and strengthen that connection and flow in us so we can overcome the challenges and heal from trauma and abuse.

We have to show up. We have to open to be vulnerable in order to create our life.

And when we show up and open up, God shows up and Grace flows.

My life has been a constant search for understanding; it has brought me around the world on so many incredible and fun adventures, and obviously some very painful ones too, leading me to explore a multitude of Traditions, Religions, Shamanism, and Philosophies, that all touched my heart and helped me to connect to God/Love, getting me through experiences that left me temporarily deeply depressed, confused, lost, hurt, and on edge of wanting to check out of this life many a time.

Through immersing myself in, and observing Nature -- its cycles, rhythms and seasons -- I have gained so much insight into my life that has helped me reconcile and heal old wounds and traumas by looking at the bigger picture. As one of my elders used to say, looking at life from the astronauts' perspective, rather than through a narrow scope.

I am so grateful and thrilled to share my story with you. It is quite a journey!

This book covers a portion of my childhood and youth in the Prologue to give some essential background information, and then focuses on a four-year period of my life where my world was turned upside down, inside out. I was challenged to know myself in new ways and go beyond the interpretations and definitions that had previously defined my life. In every Chapter I share what insights helped me through each experience, my thought processes at the time of the experiences and what gave me strength to make it through. It was a very rich, difficult, Grace-filled and enlightening time in my life. Those four years had the potential to either completely break me or make me. Fortunately it's the latter.

It is my hope that my shared experiences will inspire you to connect to Nature, to yourself and to Life in a new and life affirming way that you can see and know your worth, your value, your power and capacity to transform your life and know that you are truly so loved. All of Life and Nature is cheering you on to rise and fulfill your unique destiny and purpose. May you be open to receive that love and support that is always available to you when you choose to connect.

It is also my hope that, on some level, through recognizing our shared experiences and commonalities as human beings; that we all have pain and trauma that causes us often to feel isolated alone and that we all need and want to feel we belong and that we are enough, that my story can inspire an inner and outer movement toward connecting in our unity and growing greater kindness and compassion with all life and each other. Kindness is the way to inner and outward peace, with ourselves and with others.

Enjoy!

PROLOGUE

"Every Holy Man has a past,
And every Sinner has a future."
- unknown

My street name is Raisin, given to me the first night I hung out with the street kids and punks in downtown Toronto. I was given this name because I wore all purple: purple makeup, purple lipstick, and of course purple hair. My new street friends said they would have called me Grape, but that name was already taken by a female skinhead. I felt really cool; as if for the first time in my life I belonged. This phase of my journey was one of the most honest in my life. I say this because my hurt and anger was out in the open for the first time; I was raw and looking to be heard and seen. In a way, I had also found a kind of family there with the street kids.

My father had enrolled me in modeling school. It's for this reason that at 14 years of age, I travelled to Toronto by myself. I was about halfway through the course when I kept meeting up with these two punky kids who spent most of their time on the street, Roland and Michelle. I thought they were really cool and I wanted to meet them, so I did. I went up to them one day when I saw them on the subway again and introduced myself. They received me. That is where my journey on the streets began. It was summer, I was out of school, so when they asked me to hang out with them and the other street kids, I thought that was great so I said okay.

I got the first hint of my being really different when in the modeling school we were told to stand in front of the mirror and strike poses Vogue style as if in a photoshoot. While the others were doing all these glamor poses I was doing these wild body contortions, definitely very punk-like, alternative and wild. I thought it was great. However, the looks I got from the others was not so approving. I have to giggle out loud every time I remember that. I didn't yet have my purple hair and shaved sides, but when I look back now I could sure see it coming.

When I was nine-years-old, visiting my mom in Germany, we went to some big city where I saw my first punks. I absolutely loved them and I said to my mom, "That's what I'm going to be when I grow up," in quite a matter-of-fact way. A child's intuition I guess. She looked at me with a stern glare and said "Oh no, you're not!" I think it's the feeling of freedom and creativity that fascinated and drew me to them. They lived outside the box, and I liked that!

Well, to my rebellious mind, my mother lived on the other side of the planet, so when it happened she had no say in the matter.

My mother separated from my father when I was seven. They fought a lot and, from how I understand it now, they were both simply too young when they got married. They tried to make it work but it couldn't -- for that and other various reasons that are not necessary to go into here.

My mother had returned to Germany to visit her dying grandmother when I was eight. That's when she met this wonderful man, Rhienhold. She fell in love, got married to him after knowing him only five months. She fully moved to Germany when I was nine. That's when she flew me over for the wedding, and we went to the city where I saw the punks.

It was quite confusing how fast everything changed. I was going to a foreign country where they speak a different language that I knew nothing about and I would be meeting a man I had never met before who was going to be my step-father. In some ways though, it was exciting as well. I was going to be out of school and away from all the challenges in my life at home and school.

When I met Rheinhold I liked him instantly! He graciously took me in as his daughter without question and made me feel very welcome. He was a loving and fun-hearted man. We hit it off better than could have been imagined, which of course helped me adjust to the changes of being in a new country.

I slept a lot the first week, the time change had knocked me out and it all felt like a fantasy. When I woke up each day I had to orientate myself to where I was. Rheinhold had a really large family, so now, I suddenly had so many new cousins and aunts, etc. The wedding was beautiful, though I couldn't understand anything. My mother had made her dress and had mine made so they looked similar. I felt like a princess in it. After the wedding, I was able to connect with my new cousins and have some fun. They tried to speak English with the few words they knew and I used hand and body gestures. They received me nicely and were very curious. Aside from my mother, they had never met a Canadian before. After a very short time, I felt I had truer friends there than I did in Canada. No one teased me or bullied me, to them I was kind of like a celebrity. It felt nice.

I stayed in Germany for about three weeks. It was really beautiful. They lived directly by the Rhine river, which flowed through their back yard. I would visit that powerful river every day and marvel at its force and beauty. Because the wedding was so close to Christmas, there were also already outdoor Christmas markets happening and festivals in all the surrounding towns. Germans really know how to have a good time! It was hard for me to go back home after all that fun and good times.

After that trip I saw my mother once a year for 1 month except in my punk phase where there was almost a two-year gap. Her being so far away was hard, painful, and difficult to get used to in so many ways. I definitely suffered, feeling abandoned and left behind, which took years to heal. From my current understanding and perspective, when I look at the whole of my life and having healed my relationship with her now, I can see the definite blessings of all that happened.

One of the big blessings was that I developed sincere friendships with the kids I met in Germany every summer, something I didn't have back home. They liked and loved me. They couldn't wait to see me and wrote me letters pretty much weekly when I would go back home. This helped me get through the bullying I constantly experienced at school to which I had to return after each visit. At the same time though, it did create a split in me that created a lot of melancholy and sadness that affected all my relationships at home. But even that, too, had its blessings. Contrast creates a necessary friction that brings forth new life. It deepened my heart and soul and my search for understanding life.

The other big blessing was that her moving to Germany opened a whole new world for me in my later years -- a world that deeply resonated with my deepened soul. I was always drawn to philosophical explorations as far back as I can remember, again greatly stimulated by the traumas of my childhood. Germany has some of the best and deepest philosophers on the planet. It was pure nourishing soul food for me.

Yes, there is no happening without reason or possibility of growth, evolution and blessing. I could not have grown into who I am without all the life experiences my mother's leaving catalyzed and created in me. Her action of leaving actually liberated my soul.

* * *

There is a wisdom of Hawaii called Kina ole. As my Kahuna Elder and Teacher defines Kina Ole it means doing "The right thing, the right time, in the right way, for the right reasons, the first time."

To our western mind that sounds like a tall order that we have to work hard to fulfill. But what it actually means is that everything already is that, otherwise it would be different than what is or was. It's a deep understanding and acceptance that life is bigger than us and that all things have their reason, place and purpose. It's up to us to open our awareness to connect it all and harvest the hidden blessings and wisdoms.

*   *   *

My father worked a lot and usually came home after my sister and I were in bed and often left before we got up, so in my time on the streets I did one of two things: either I snuck out to catch the last train downtown or I lied and said I was staying at a friend's. He never checked. So later on when he found out that I had been hanging out on the streets, sleeping in stairwells and hotel bathrooms or all-night clubs and was also panhandling on the street corners, it was really shocking for him. Understandably.

For me it was fun, spending time with the kids I met. I had finally found my clan after being an outcast all the years before. Fortunately the street scene back then in the1980's wasn't as rough as it is today, there were only a handful of us and we ranged from freaks, Goths, Punks, and Skinheads, so everyone pretty much tolerated each other, looked out for each other, more or less. Fights only happened when someone did something, not just because of the differences.

I was also lucky that I knew the Skinhead leader. He had attended my school the year before and we had become friends, so I was protected. Nothing bad ever happened to me, thankfully. I was on the streets most of the summer. I sometimes stayed at my friend's Darius' house and a friend of mine, Dee Dee's, at her uncle's house. Nights when we stayed at the all-night club called the Twilight Zone, we also often snuck into a local hotel bathroom and plugged in our crimping irons, refreshing ourselves for the day, doing our makeup and such in the early hours of the morning.

A few times we did milk runs where we would take the bread and milk delivery from the hotel that was dropped off at the back door. We had fun together; though we each had our hurts and hardships, it all disappeared when we hung out. We had created our own little bubble to escape reality.

In the winter I frequented the street still, though not as much as in the summer. I skipped school so often that in the Fall when I was 15, the principal called me to his office and threatened to kick me out of school. I broke down and told him of my situation. He showed compassion and hooked me up with the guidance counselor of the high school. The counselor was a bit freaked out by my black wardrobe, (I had transitioned from purple to black) my Souzie and the Banshee makeup and curiosity of exploring witchcraft, or more accurately, the Wiccan tradition. His discomfort was palpable in the room each time. But nonetheless through our sessions, it came to light just how much anger there was in me toward my mother for leaving me. I discovered that I had successfully suppressed those feelings because of my need to receive her love. My mind was blown open to how we can have a different reality in our subconscious that we have no idea about until we see it. Also how those unknown factors wreak havoc in our life and relationships. I am very grateful for the principal of my school seeing my distress and supporting me through those sessions.

A boiling point came that Christmas, after yet another family fight and the loss of a small job I had maintained all that time. I attempted to take my life. I had just reached a limit and had so much pain that had been unearthed that a part of me didn't want to go on. I tried to reach out to the counselor but he didn't return my calls. I understand the altered reality one enters into when feeling suicidal, and I know how hard it is once it gets hold of you, to not give into it. I tried, by taking a handful of sleeping pills I had stolen from my fathers sock drawer. At the time I was living in a basement suite with a friend in her family's home. She saw me and called an ambulance after I had locked myself in the bathroom to take the pills. I put them in my mouth, drank the water, and broke down into wailing tears while looking at myself in the mirror. Then I heard a voice saying "It doesn't have to be this way." Whether it was an angel, which I believe it was, or my own mind, that statement woke me out of the suicide trance I was in. I vomited the pills back up, unlocked the bathroom door, and curled up in a ball in the corner, and sobbed deeply until the ambulance and my father showed up. From that day, I went back home, started rebuilding myself, and stopped going to the streets.

You may be asking how did all this come to be? How did the 14-year-old girl I was have so much trauma that she ended up on the streets and nearly taking her life at 15? How did no one catch on, see what was happening?

*　*　*

There was a heavy cloud of trauma in my family that was never addressed or dealt with. That trauma lead to some major numbness and dysfunction; pretty much every day there was fighting going on. My mother separated from my father when I was 7 as I mentioned, and my sister, Lorri, was 12. At that time, my mom's leaving was in itself, a devastation to all of us. Then, a few months later, Lorri had a near-fatal horseback riding accident when competing in a jumping competition. She was clinically dead for one minute, and when she came back she was in a coma for several months. My whole life changed. All of our lives changed. Again.

I remember I had been playing in the back of the stables where Lorri's competition was, looking for frogs with the other kids when I heard my friend Lisa, who came with us to watch Lori's jumping competition, calling me to hurry up and come, that my sister had fallen off her horse. I ran as fast as I could and pushed my way through the people and saw her lying there motionless. I wanted to run to her but someone grabbed me and held me back until my father finally noticed and told them to let me come through. I ran to her in tears, sat by her side and saw the blood coming out of her ear. The ambulance finally came and I went home with Lisa.

A part of me died that day. Everything in me just collapsed. My soul retreated out of this world. It was all just too much for my little heart and mind to understand so much loss. First my mother, now Lorri.

When I remember the joy in my heart, the naturalness of me while playing with the kids chasing frogs, I realize that that had been the last time I had ever felt so free until much later in life. That is when my innocence was fully interrupted and my spirit was broken. There were already other family issues and traumatic experiences prior to that, so this just compounded everything. Until that moment there had been what I call a metaphorical inner elastic band I had that was flexible enough to help me bounce back from those other issues. After this though, losing my mother and sister within six months of each other, the elastic broke. From that day I was dissociated and lived in my own bubble. My cognitive abilities weakened and a false identity started being created as a way to cope. I became hidden, shy, started lying, and I created fantasy realities to escape into. I was in a state of absolute shock.

I stopped being creative and never did well in school after that. I was always zoning out and could never retain information. Nowadays if that were to happen the teachers and doctors would identify it as post-traumatic stress. They would pay more attention to all the signals indicating something was terribly wrong and give me support.

But back then in the 1970's, people didn't know. I was expected to carry on as if nothing happened. It was the era where things like this were swept under the rug, avoided, and glazed over. So instead of being helped to understand what was happening, I was treated as if I was stupid. My school even put me in special needs classes.

Since my mom lived in an apartment in Toronto, for a year and a half before she moved to Germany, and because my father was either at work or at the hospital with Lorri for close to a year, I was shuffled from neighbor to neighbor. This speaks highly for the level of community that existed then, but for me I had just lost everything I knew to be my life, and no one paid attention. I was an extra burden for each of these families, and I felt it. I was and felt very alone and lost. I became numb. I lost all the enthusiasm and joy I had known before. School became a nightmare; I was bullied and teased daily, being told I had a cripple for sister, cruel jokes about her were spread through the school and all kinds of other nightmarish garbage. I wanted to disappear. One saving grace and joy was when my grandma sometimes would come and take care of me at the house, which was nice, because I could be at home.

It was quite a while before my parents would let me see Lorri in the hospital. For me it was as if she had just vanished, as if she had never existed. When I did see her for the first time since the accident she was skin and bones with black eyes and was being fed intravenously. It was a scary sight. She was in a coma for several months. When she finally started emerging from it, she was in a very violent and aggressive state. The first word she spoke to me was fuck you. She would repeatedly call me to her, I would run to her happy and hopeful to talk to her. She would tell me to come closer, then would scream at me, "Fuck you!" Again and again and again.

More confusion, more pain. I would run out of her room crying to my mother in the waiting room. My mother stayed with her at the hospital most of the time; she tried to tell me that Lorri didn't mean it, but it didn't take the effect away. Lorri always had a bit of a jealous and mean streak in her toward me since as far back as I could remember. She often brutally teased me with her friends, all the while laughing at me. So it was hard for me to believe my mom when she said Lorri didn't mean it. But I loved her and always wanted her approval of me in some way to feel she loved me, too.

I also always felt inferior to her. She had been an amazing artist, great at sports, had lots of friends, and was really smart in school. I felt intimidated to even attempt to do any of the things she excelled at for fear of not being good enough, not wanting to be compared. Because of those dynamics we were never really close but close enough that I cared for her and I was really sad about what had happened.

It was a long healing process for her. She had to learn to walk, talk, eat, write, everything like a child again. The doctors told her she would never walk again or be able to draw. She had been an amazing artist, when she drew animals she really caught their spirit, they looked alive and real. They also said she would never ride horses again, which had been her absolute passion.

Over the next two years she did prove the doctors wrong on many counts. She did everything they told her she wouldn't -- and completed college as well. Her mental health, however, was very fragile. When she finally came home she was completely different from before. She was always angry. Particularly with me. Though she always had a bit of a temper before, she was more aggressive and reacted to the smallest things. She would bang her head against the wall, try to pull her hair out and had emotional attacks that were terrifying to watch. Once she actually almost strangled me; I was blue in the face when she finally let go. It didn't take much to set her off. Even if I peed too loud in the bathroom that was on the opposite side of her bedroom she would bang on the wall and yell at me to be quiet. It was hell living at home with her.

This is all natural behavior for someone who has gone through what she did with her head injuries, but I didn't understand it. All I felt was that she hated me and was always mean to me and I didn't understand why. It wasn't easy at all. She was a total stranger to me.

She eventually went back to school where she encountered her own challenges of being rejected by her old friends because she now walked with a slight limp. This of course only compounded her already-fragile nervous system and it was all discharged on me. I was the scapegoat on which to vent her hurt and frustration. Of course as an adult now I know she couldn't help it, but to the little girl I was, her hostility left an imprint in me that caused a myriad of distortions and coping mechanisms to develop that set up the basic blueprint of my formed identity and my relationship to the world.

Somewhere, through all this, I adopted the belief that I must have done something really wrong or be really bad that Mom left and Lorri was so mean to me. My psychology built itself around that foundational belief system. I created coping mechanisms and convinced myself that I understood them both and why they were as they were, when I really didn't. I had simply convinced myself of that as a way to avoid feeling the pain and loneliness. I just wanted to be loved and so I repressed the raw feelings of hurt, and took on the role of caregiver in many ways, putting other people's needs and feelings ahead of my own. I also needed to be the strong one, which blocked the natural expression of what I was feeling and going through. The following years were really hard, especially because our mother was gone, our Father was always at work and Lorri had to somehow take on the role of caregiver for me, her younger sister. It was a role she was in no way capable of and should not have been put in. She still needed to heal from so much and her emotional sensitivity actually was getting worse. How could it not, with the pressure of having to be a mom for me. So many layers.

It was at the age of 14 that I started really searching deeply, trying on different ways of expression, trying to understand basically everything about my life. I searched for God and tried to understand my family dynamics. My life felt like a mess, and there was a lot stirring in my subconscious that needed to be expressed and released, hence my punk phase emerged, lifting the lid off the pressure cooker that had been boiling under the surface.

In spite of all the tumultuous emotions, anger and pain, I would always find temporary reprieve in Nature. We lived down the street from a small forest park and a beach on Lake Ontario. My heart connected to a set of rocks that were at the edge of the water. They became my temple. I would sometimes sit on them for hours, no matter the weather, even in the winter. I would question life and I would cry and let it all out. I was searching for something: God, Angels, Nature Spirits, to soothe and heal my heart. The existence of "other worldly" support was always a natural possibility and awareness for me.

The sound of the waves would almost hypnotize me. I felt at peace. My nervous system could unwind. Sunsets would warm my heart and put me in a state of awe and wonder at the beauty of life and nature. Sunsets stimulated hope in me. This was my first experience and realization of the healing power of Nature.

After I had gone home after my suicide attempt I spent a lot of time with my rocks, and I loved going on the swing at the park near the forest. It was soothing for me. I still don't have many memories of that following year, except reading a lot and going into Nature. It was just a year of readjustment, finding my way back into life.

At 17 I went to a personal-development oriented modeling school, John Casablancas. That really helped raise my confidence and get me back into life. I also met a girl there who became my best friend. We had so much fun together, as she loved Nature too. She was my sister "Sag," because we were both Sagittarians. Though there was still so much buried in me, I came back to life. There was joy in me again. The ghosts of my past remained hidden until the time period I will be sharing following this chapter. I modeled for almost two years. I did more than 300 fashion shows in that time and was the house model for Joico Canada hair products in Toronto. It was a lot of fun, and was a great bridge for me back into life.

Meanwhile, my sister, after successfully graduating from college, tried working in a company for graphic design. Because of the accident she was still hyper sensitive and couldn't navigate both the stress of working in the company and the often nonsense gossip that happens at work places that she felt was going on behind her back. She always felt people were laughing at her because of her limp. There was still so much unresolved trauma and pain, which unfortunately opened the door for alcohol. She stepped out of living and isolated herself more and more. When not healed, traumas grow and can become distorted when there is substance abuse, making it even harder to get to the true source of it all. When I think of her I see in my mind's eye an ancient beautiful castle that has massive thorny vines and bushes covering it, protecting and hiding it from the world. And it's like, though the initial creation of them was to protect, to create a safe space, they have become entangled even more with the unhealed wounds and the stories and distortions created by the influence of alcohol. It feels as if she is now trapped, but does not see she is trapped. She has cut out of her life her friends and family and is alone. But in the end who's to say? As with Kinaole, even though we cannot know why some people and things are as they are, what they are is clearly with purpose and reason, otherwise it would not be, and we have the option to trust the soul of life behind it all. Learning to let go and hold space around this has been a really hard challenge for me, that I am getting better at navigating ... but who am I to say she should live and be different? I hold a candle of light for her in my heart always.

* * *

In September, 1989, I flew the Germany to stay with my mom and my step father Rheinhold. I hadn't completed high school yet but I had a feeling to go. I ended up staying with her for only a month and went on to move to a neighboring town to do a practicum in a five-star hotel to be a restauranteur for almost a year. In that time I visited many beautiful places of Nature that opened my heart so much. Everything always felt better in Nature!

Behind our home there was a little mountain that also had a long trail that went deep into a valley. One day I walked for hours in the fog. It was so mystical and beautiful. I couldn't say why, but I felt transformed when I returned. Then I went to the Alps in Switzerland with my mom and Rheinhold. When I got to the top and saw the majesty and beauty I couldn't stop crying. I was in absolute awe. It touched my soul in an unknown place. Again I felt transformed. I felt deeply humbled and immensely grateful for life. I also felt a greater power up there, call it God/ Spirit, there was no doubt in me of there being a higher force governing all of creation.

Another beautiful place that affected me and woke up my soul was the Wutachschlucht. It's an area in the Black Forest, full of waterfalls, creeks, beautiful trees and hiking trails you can walk for hours. I felt childlike joy and playfulness awaken in me. My connection to Nature increased a thousand-fold. Where I lived in the hotel staff house, we were near a lake in the forest that I would walk and ride my bicycle around, often bringing a little picnic for myself. It's such a beautiful place.

I was in heaven! I feel that spending all that time in nature healed me in ways nothing else could.

I developed amazing friendships working in the Hotel. I had so much fun there. It was the teen years I should have had back home. I am eternally grateful for that time in my life. It strengthened me, and I see now how it prepared me for the trials to come.

During my time at that hotel I received a job offer in the Italian part of Switzerland. At the last minute I had joined a friend of mine when she drove there for a job interview. It was completely by chance that I went with her; I was supposed to be doing something else but my other friend cancelled, making me available to join her! Another serendipity that changed my life.

When we drove into Tessin my heart leaped and said "I want to live here!" It was so beautiful, the mountains, the lake, the palm trees and tropical flowers you would never imagine to be in Switzerland. The hotel was up this precariously narrow road up the mountain overlooking Lago Maggiore. Breathtaking! We pulled in and met the owners and they gave us a really nice suite for the two days we were staying. We had some fun adventures and ate so much delicious food. I felt so at home there and just wanted to stay.

A week after we returned to Germany she was told she got the job! We had been roommates until then, and I was sad to see her go, but very happy for her. Amazingly one month later they asked her to ask me if I would like to work there, too. That was a no-brainer! I gave notice and my friends had a massive farewell surprise party for me. I felt so loved and grateful for all my friends there. I would miss them but I was so excited for my new adventure! Off I went a few weeks later.

Living in Europe gave me a new lease on life. I still had buried residues of my childhood traumas and patterns that had governed my life until then, but I was happy and creating a new life for myself away from all the history. Away from everything and everyone that held me back. Everything happened like magic.

My first year in Switzerland working in the hotel in Brissago was quite an experience. When I went for a walk one day I found an abandoned church that was built on a cliff with a stream flowing under it. This became one of my sacred Nature places to retreat to and commune with nature, God/Spirit. I started exploring writers like Hermann Hesse, Goethe, Plato, Socrates, going deep into self-discovery. Also spiritual books on earth-based religions, meditation etc., All of that, unbeknownst to me, was also preparing me for the turbulence of the years to come.

There is an expression you may have also heard before, "Be Careful What you Pray For or Ask For." I was praying with all my might to heal, understand, and grow. I got what I asked for, just differently from what I anticipated. This is where my story of the four-year marathon of trying to survive the many knocks, twists and turns begins. Here we go....

1

THE CALL TO A NEW LIFE

"She hears the cry. Feels the sensation.
The power is in the air.
Such a strong and positive force.
She opens to it.
It embraces her.
"Her heart and soul absorbs into the universe.
The divine is there.
With wings of beauty and protection, awaiting her arrival.
"She attempts to reach it.
It seems to move further away. She pushes her way through,
determined to make it.
"She arrives.
"Basking in the warm glow of this spirit.
She emanates in its energy and experiences the ecstasy of life
Rushing through her veins like a drug.
"She wants to cry for joy,
The joy of feeling such bliss,
Within herself,
Within her world.
"A single tear is shed.
And with this tear she begins to shed her insecurities and
negative ways."
- Journal Entry, Feb.10, 1991

It's December 31st 1990. I was visiting my family back home in Pickering, Ontario after having lived in Europe for almost two years. It was a strange experience being back. My time away had changed me in incredible ways. Living in a different culture, learning and speaking a new language, I felt different and estranged from my family and the life I knew before I left for Germany. Another big difference was that a year after I had moved to Europe my mother left Rheinhold and had moved back to Pickering. I had an ongoing joke for many years that she was always running away from me. It felt strange that she was there now too. Nonetheless, I was happy to visit and reconnect.

I lost connection with most of the friends I had before going to Germany. I reached out to some of them but aside from one, I didn't meet anyone. One place I was looking forward to was visiting Downtown Toronto. I had a favorite cafe on Yonge Street that I used to frequent in my punk days called The Living Well Café. It was one of the all-night places my friends and I would hang out at. I continued going there through my modeling phase, as well. It was an alternative, funky environment and they had great food.

A few days after I arrived, feeling suffocated at home, I needed to get out of the house so I caught the GO Train and headed downtown. I liked being there; it was where I had my first taste of independence. I also liked the diversity of cultures that Toronto represents.

I had lunch, which was super yummy and I ordered my favorite Chocolate Pecan Pie. While I was waiting for it I went to the magazine stand to find something to read. I had spotted a New Age Magazine about meditation etc., so while I enjoyed my pie, I leafed through it and found out about a World Healing Meditation event that was happening on New Year's Day at 6 a.m. at the Kensington Market in downtown Toronto. I felt an instant desire to go. It felt like what I now call inner guidance. It feels like a warm inner tug, like a magnetic force pulling me.

I decided I would go.

Having always been a seeker, trying to find my way and sense of place in the world and with my deep love of Nature, I thought this would be a nice experience to meet like-minded people. I felt excited and was really looking forward to it.

I never really felt like I fit in at home. There was always this underlying tension that made being in the house uncomfortable. I went for many walks to my rocks at the Lake. Nature being my greatest ally and source of peace, the tension would just wash away.

My father didn't understand why I wanted to go back to Europe. He kept telling me I was wasting my time and my life. that I should come back home and finish school. The thought of living there again constricted my soul completely. There was no way that was going to happen. I couldn't imagine it. So that became an ongoing battle with him, for years and years, to fight for my rights to be me and find my own way.

You see, my dad and I were and are very different. He is all about safety and security, pure logic. That is how he has navigated his life, and it works for him. But for me, I'm the gypsy, inspired to explore, take risks and create my life in a more dynamic and colorful way. The clashing energy between us was intense. He was very loving too, and a great father in every other way, but in that regard, it was a constant source of strain on our relationship.

One day I went downtown again and came across a CD store that was looking for part-time help. I thought that would be great, I can make some money, get out of the house and be where I liked to be. I went in and applied and they hired me on the spot. It was a lot of fun and served me well the remaining months I was visiting until my return to Switzerland in May.

New Year's Eve came around pretty fast.

That evening my sister Lorri had her boyfriend over for dinner and drinks. I invited Chris, an old high-school crush of mine, to join us. The night was quickly going by as we toasted the New Year with champagne hugs and kisses; then we just hung out together in the living room listening to music. I think we watched a movie, too.

It was already 4:30 in the morning when I looked at the clock, I had lost track of time. If I wanted to make the World Healing Meditation event I had to leave soon.

I thought about it for a few moments. I was tired and had more to drink than usual so I rationalized that I can tune in to the World Meditation from home. That decision lasted maybe 10 minutes when I suddenly felt this sensation in my gut, an inner tug of energy. I felt almost an urgency that I had to go, that it wasn't enough to just go to my room and tune in at 6 a.m.

I always had a certain kind of sensitivity or intuition as far back as I can remember. I would just sense and know things. I was learning to trust those sensations and intuitions.

I decided to put the effort in to try to make it.

I decided to trust the inner tug.

Excited, I went to my friend Chris, and asked him if he could quickly take me to the GO train that was leaving at 5 a.m. Fortunately the Go Train was only 10 minutes away by car. He grumbled a bit, said I was crazy, as everyone in my family thought I was, but got ready and drove me as quickly as he could. I just barely made it and the train pulled away.

I was excited and curious what I would encounter. I suddenly felt as if I had drunk several cups of coffee. My body was buzzing.

All my life I had hid my spiritual side from my family and most people. It was my secret life. Now I was going to meet others with a similar path. How amazing!

* * *

I experienced my first sense of what you might call a spiritual force of love and good, call it God or Spirit if you will, when I was seven years old. It was after the traumas in my family happened. I was watching T.V. one day in our living room when I stumbled on a show talking about Jesus. I didn't have a religious upbringing, but my grandma had a Bible and I heard his name mentioned many a time. In the T.V. show the person talking said all we had to do was call on Jesus and he would come help us. I sat there crying and asked Jesus to help me, take away my hurt and heal my family.

I did as the man said. As I called on Jesus, I felt a warmth enfold me. I felt an energy of love and care. It was surprising and beautiful. I stopped crying and somehow felt less alone. Even though I couldn't read well, the next time I was at my grandma's I asked her for her Bible that I knew was about Jesus. She gave it to me, though surprised by my request. I kept it under my pillow as a way to feel connected to the energy I had experienced. I really feel that experience helped me, gave me a sense of hope and connection to something Greater. Though I know for many, there is a lot of disbelief about the spiritual aspect of life, that it is all fantasy and "new age" nonsense, I always felt connected to something intangible, ineffable. I think we get too caught up in the name of that force of good and love that is real, that we have all felt at some point or other, that we lose touch with the energy itself. Instead of tuning in to it and letting those benevolent forces guide us, we waste our time arguing about the name, or which religion is the "only" right one. A very detrimental distraction indeed.

As I grew older I would go to many friends different churches, looking for that feeling, even something close to it, but never found it. Everything was about sin and fear. So I started exploring other religions, traditions, and philosophies to understand what I had experienced. I found that the nature-based traditions resonated with me most.

I started exploring meditation when I was 12, I would meditate staring at candle light because it really relaxed me and put me in an altered state of awareness. At 13 I became acquainted with Pagan and Druid traditions through a book called *Drawing Down the Moon* that spoke to my heart deeply. I found a partial reflection of what I felt when I was 7 reflected in those teachings. They were very connected to Nature and were based on Goddess traditions, focusing on the Divine Feminine. That was a new way of approaching understanding the cycles of life and Nature. For me it was beautiful! I found it filled a big gap in the approach to spirituality, bringing feminine energy in to balance the masculine. Somehow it gave me a sense of place and purpose in this world. Historically, in the "olden" days of religion the feminine aspect had an important role as well, but had gotten lost in man's search for power and control. With that, we lost the ability to see all life as sacred. We lost sight of the oneness of all creation, how it and we are all connected. The yielding and feeling aspect of the feminine was deemed weak and so it was rejected. That is the message I got growing up, that women were silly and emotional with no common sense. Not to be taken seriously. It was so nice to have a different option on how to relate to being a woman.

I was so touched by these teachings of the Divine Feminine that I started identifying myself as a Pagan and I prayed to both God and Goddess. I started doing a self- blessing ritual that was in the book *Drawing Down the Moon*. The first time I did it, this swell of emotion poured out of me. I cried and cried. It was as if this ceremony opened a portal in me that was holding all this emotion and it finally had a way to get out of my body. After the tears subsided, I felt a peace growing in me. A rested calm. It felt like a homecoming. This prayer blessing became my stronghold all of the years to come. It gave me a positive focus to which to direct my attention, particularly when I felt, sad, lost or confused. I believe it is what brought me through my experience on the streets. No matter how angry I was in that phase, I never lost touch with that part of me that connected to Nature. I continued to do that ceremony almost daily until my 20's. That is when my world started expanding in other spiritual directions. Having this sense of connection to Nature, God/dess, helped me cope with the loss, grief, and anger that was still buried in me.

When I was 14 I read Joseph Campbell's book, *The Power of Myth*. It really nourished me. I found it fascinating reading about archetypes, how they shape our understanding of ourselves and life. He emphasized that we should follow our own bliss, meaning to find our unique way through life to fulfillment. That resonated deep in me. It fed my natural rebelliousness to be who and how I choose to be, not what society said I should be. He touched on the Feminine archetypes too, which gave more validation to my explorations with the divine feminine.

That same year I had my first experience of Native American teachings; they touched my heart deeply, with their love and reverence to Nature. And their value of the feminine was a match for my heart.

One day when I was watching T.V. I came across a Canadian-produced movie about the history of Native Americans and Residential Schools.

It was done as a story, revolving around a young girl who had been taken away from her family and put into a residential school. They later told her that her entire family had died. Something in her told her that it wasn't true. She could feel her family was still alive. The children were treated terribly, as we know, and were forbidden to speak their native language.

The girl befriended another girl at the school. In secret they would meet and talk in their native language with each other. Then one night she went to her new friend and they snuck out and went to the stables. She had just started her moon time, her monthly cycle, and wanted to do a ceremony with her friend to welcome it, as was custom in their tradition. It was beautiful; I cried and felt found. Prior to starting my cycle I had felt a joy, like it was something special. I even knew the day before it was going to start. I told my Dad that I thought it was going to happen the next day. He said impossible, I was only 12. Well the next day I did start my first cycle.

Unfortunately though, from that moment on, I was told it's a terrible thing, from my sister and others at school. They called it a curse and other such negative references, making me feel dirty for having my period. I felt confused. I imagined it being celebrated. I don't know why I imagined that, but I did. So when I saw the scene where the girls were celebrating entering womanhood, where they even painted each other with blood to welcome this next phase of her life, my heart melted. The sadness I had held around my experience came out of me and I replaced it with joy and gratitude. I celebrated with them. That is what connected me to Native Cultures and opened my curiosity to explore them more later in life.

* * *

On the way downtown to the World Healing Meditation I was remembering and reflecting on these memories. I knew there would be a Native Elder at this event smoking the peace pipe. I was so excited. I had been alone on my spiritual explorations for so long; now I felt like a child going to a candy store!

Little did I know the magnitude that this seemingly small action of choosing to go, would redirect my life trajectory.

Every day we make choices, little ones, or big ones, and we often take for granted the impact these choices have on our lives. We don't realize the power we have to create the momentum of our coming days weeks and years, simply by our ability to choose one thing, one action, over another. It's a constant dance as long as we live, each choice opening different pathways that lead us to different things, places and outcomes.

This choice opened me to my heart and soul path, to the people and experiences that created opportunities and space for me to go beyond the self that was created as a reaction to life. I started living from my soul, from my deepest inklings of insights and dreams that had been buried within me. It opened a door that quite likely would not have opened without my having shown up that day.

So here I was, I had just turned 20 and I was on this mystical journey downtown, walking into the unknown. So exciting!

I arrived just moments before it began. I found myself a seat among the hundreds of people close to the middle. Once everyone had settled, we were invited to sing healing songs from different cultures. As I began to sing I felt a warm energy flood my body, and my heart opened. I felt connected to me, to my soul. I felt joy. I felt hope. I felt found. My voice also opened as it never had before. I had always wanted to be a singer when I was little, but I got teased and was told I couldn't sing, so the jokes and comments sealed that dream shut inside of me, until that day. It felt so good, I just wanted to keep singing.

I was absolutely elated. The event went on with elders and other people speaking about how peace begins with us. They gave us direction for when the moment came that we would join the World Meditation that was happening around the world simultaneously for four minutes of silent prayer. It was like nothing I had experienced before. I felt so alive, so optimistic of my future. Like a whole new world opened up before me, and in me. There were others who felt this kind of connection to Nature, to Spirit, just like me! So many! How thrilling! I was absolutely glowing with joy!

When it was over I stood to wait to exit my row. At one point, my eyes met those of a girl my age about six rows up from me. We smiled at each other. As I made it out of my row and headed to the exit we ended up standing beside each other.

We smiled and said hello. Then I felt that same energetic tug, nudging me to connect more with her. So I just blurted, "Hey do you want to go get a coffee together?" She said sure, that would be great! I had never done anything like that before. Though I enjoyed meeting new people I was not usually that forward. I think a part of me also wanted to extend my experience as long as I could before going back home, as well as make a new friend. I was changing every moment. I really surprised myself.

We went to a coffee shop on Yonge St., and shared a bit about our spiritual paths. Her name was Gennie. How cool it was, a part of me thought. There is someone I can share this part of me with what everyone else thinks is weird. The amazing thing to me was that she was really touched and impressed with my views, thoughts, and practices. She wanted to hear more. Until then I had only known one other person I could talk to about this stuff. I had modeled and lived with that friend in Toronto until I left for Germany. Though we didn't connect at the same depth as Gennie and I were in just our first conversation, she had some understanding and awareness because her mother was a modern-day witch. We had been really good friends. We lost touch though when she pursued her career modeling and acting in Hollywood. She had a huge impact on my life, as she introduced me to the book *The Prophet* by Kahlil Gibran. She read me the whole book the night before my flight to Germany to calm me and reduce my fear. I was so nervous. The writings in this book matched my heart's knowing so much that I bought a copy the next morning before catching my flight. I have it to this day. It became my spiritual resource, for guidance and remembrance. It's like a Bible to me. I shared that with Gennie, too. She knew the book as well. Amazing! We were so on the same page.

Gennie and I talked for several hours, and the time just flew by. We exchanged numbers and made vague plans of when we would meet again. I went home so happy, but when I entered the house I always felt I had to shut that part of me down, which added to the tension that was always there. My family never really saw me. They were always telling me I should be something other than what I was. My mother and sister made fun of my interest in philosophy and spirituality. My dad always criticized me that I bought too many books. It was frustrating. Why wouldn't anyone just let me be me? Why did I have to fill everyone's ideas and expectations of me when no one did that for me and no one took the time to know me? So my protective masks erected again to keep my heart safe. I know and knew on some level they loved and cared for me in their own way, but, I often questioned who is the "me" they thought I was. I just never felt met and seen. Fortunately that has changed.

I wanted to meet with Gennie again as soon as possible; I could only stand being at home so much, so I called and we arranged to meet the next day. We hung out and she invited me to stay with her at her place, which was a co-op. I ended up pretty much living there the rest of my stay and met some amazing people. Gennie took me to my first Goddess Workshop led by Kathleen Graham, who had a boa constrictor that she danced with; it was incredible. At the end of the ceremony Kathleen played her crystal singing bowls, which I had never heard before. She guided us to tone with her and the bowls. It was pure magic! I felt bliss in my body. The regular world just melted away. I felt so blessed and was so grateful for all the magic unfolding for me.

My voice opened again so beautifully I didn't recognize myself. And there was that deep warm energy in my chest spreading through my body. It was ecstatic. I felt so high after that and wanted to do and learn more. For me this young woman, Gennie, opened my world to the world I had always searched for. She was a key-holder, opening the door to my new life. We were like instant sisters. I felt seen and under-stood and so welcomed by her and everyone at the co-op. I met many other people through her who also who became instrumental in my evolution and healing.

What an adventure I was on! I can still feel the fire and joy in me as I write this. Some things just stay with you as if no time has passed.

One day I was with my friend Bill, hanging out down-town after work at the CD shop. We were walking toward the turnstile of the subway when I got that energetic tug sensation again. Gennie had told me about this woman who healed with crystals. That she had beautiful shop down by Spadina Avenue.

From the moment she told me about her I knew I wanted to meet her but just hadn't felt the urge or made the effort yet to go to her store. With a feeling of urgency again, just like the morning of the healing meditation, I just had to go right then in that moment. I told Bill and he looked at me oddly and said "There she goes," chuckling to himself. "See you later then." He knew that spontaneous part of me. He teased me sometimes too, but in a loving way.

Off I went back onto the subway. I got off at Queen and Spadina Station, I swear it was as if I had a fire in my butt quickening my stride to get me there as fast as I could. I have to chuckle when I remember myself then. I have always defi-nitely danced to the beat of my own drum! I was so earnest and eager to learn and understand everything. I had an insatiable curiosity. I am grateful for who I was then. I could have made many other choices. I could have been shut down by my pains and traumas, but it only made me more committed to learn all that I could to heal.

I arrived at the front of the building where the Crystal Store was. I was presented with a very intimidating, large flight of stairs to conquer before reaching her. I climbed with all my might. As I walked into the store, totally out of breath, I saw her and I blurted, "I don't have any idea about crystals or anything but I want to understand my life and I want to learn and heal the problems in my family." And with that I burst into uncontrollable sobs.

Iona, a woman who would fit in Avalon, gracious and beautiful, came from behind the counter and took me in her arms as I cried from such a deep place inside me. She then proceeded to hand me a crystal, a lepidolite with pink tourmaline. She said it would help calm me and bring healing to my heart. As I held it I decided to sit down, upon which time the knee in my jeans tore open. That caused us to break into laughter. How appropriate that it ripped open just like something within me had ripped open, too. Creating space to breathe and be. That touch of humor was the perfect medicine!

I started visiting Iona every day for the remainder of time I was in Toronto. She taught me about crystals, energy healing, and meditation. I spent so much money on crystals! Everything she shared felt familiar to me. It all made sense and resonated as true. She became my first spiritual mentor. She ended up being a life-line for me down the road when things got really tough. Always encouraging me, seeing my heart and my light.

Another person I met in my time in Toronto was an older man named Andre. He was a master astrologer and deep into the study of occult wisdoms, Egyptian mythology, and spirituality. He actually owned the New Age magazine I had read about the World Healing Meditation in. What a serendipity. I felt a good connection with him; we spent quite a bit of time together too before I left, and as with Iona, the owner of the Crystal store, he also became a friend and mentor.

* * *

One morning when I opened the CD store for the first time alone, something amazing happened. It was a part of our opening process to look for a CD to play that would also play outside for people walking by. As I was looking through the box that I had gone through many times before, a CD caught my eyes that I had never seen.

It was by the group called *Dead Can Dance*. I thought what an odd name. The picture on the cover was of an old mythical and mystical painting image of a woman. It intrigued me and woke up my curiosity to hear it. Well, when it started playing I got goosebumps through my whole body and an energy rush of joy exploded in me. I think my cheeks actually were flushed. It was like nothing I had ever heard before. I was so excited to discover this music. It has a sound similar to Gregorian chanting, but it's done with "vocables," sounds that the lead singer is inspired to sing in the moment. It is similar to how they sing in Native Cultures. Pure magic!

With my discovery of my voice again that CD became my inspiration to do the same as a form of meditation. To just sound out vowels and tones, whatever felt good at the time as a practice of meditation and healing. When Gordie, the manager, came to work I asked him where that CD came from, that I hadn't seen it before. He said it was his and he had forgotten it the night before. Wow. Serendipity at work again. Had he not forgotten it, another whole new world would not have opened in me. Little did I know that many years later, that would lead me to producing my own CD, singing the way I was inspired to from that CD. One action. One Choice. Chance or Destiny? My life is filled with so many magical moments like that.

One day when Andre and I were visiting, I shared my singing with him. He looked at me with big eyes and said, "Someone needs to record this." Really? I thought to myself can it be possible that it sounds as good as it feels? I was over the moon with joy for that feedback. Singing this way became my new language of prayer to connect to my heart and life's heart.

* * *

Gennie and I spent a lot of time together over the next weeks. When I was getting ready to go back to Switzerland, she set up a space for us to meditate. She put on this music that later she told me was from India. Again. Until that day I had never heard this music before but it felt so familiar to my soul and my body when I heard it. I knew nothing of India or how they meditate. While I was sitting there cross-legged across from Gennie, I felt an energy pulling me to raise my arms over my head while my hands were in prayer position. It felt really good. I actually felt a surge of energy rush through my body. Astounded, Gennie looked at me and asked me what made me do that. I said, "I don't know. The music made me do it. It just felt like this is what my body wanted to do." Then she told me that what I did is a meditation position in India. I was like wow! So many new discoveries and experiences. I was more excited than I had ever been before.

So many new worlds had opened up to me that enabled me to discover me, who I was, in those few months. Mind blowing! I was realizing just how different I had always been, and it suddenly made sense why I didn't fully fit in anywhere until then.

Now I had my own little community of friends I could share and talk with. What a gift that was. Even more so over the coming years.

I was looking forward to my new job in Switzerland. The first thing I was going to do was find a crystal and metaphysical store, to keep learning and meet more people. Until meeting Gennie, I had no idea such stores existed. The adventure would continue.

2

FOLLOWING THE FLOW

"Things In Myself to Transform and Enhance:"
1. To accept and dispel the fears that are hanging on to me and holding me back from advancing further with my spirituality and learning

2. Most important, to accept myself for who I am in every aspect. And stop being so critical of myself.

3.To release all the anger that has been built up in me over my lifetime, to face it and transform it into positive, loving energy to make me stronger.

4.To not be so critical toward the people around me, to accept them for who they are and not use what I may see against them. To know they are exactly where they are meant to be, to help me understand that fact and live with that knowledge daily."
- Journal Entry, May 1991, Ascona Switzerland, 20 Years old

Rheinhold picked me up at the airport in Zurich. Even though my mother had left him, he was always there for me. His home was just across the border in Germany in a sweet little town called Bonndorf. It was nice being back in that house and being able to visit my "mountain" that is a short walk away from his home. I have my Nature refuges everywhere I ever went and lived, where I could connect and replenish my heart and soul. Nature is the absolute panacea, natural cure, for everything that ails us. I claim this as my experience and observation in the world.

I really loved this house. My mother and he had completely gutted and renovated it into a magical and beautiful place. I was happy to stay there for a few days before venturing into my new experiences awaiting me.

For the first time in my life I was going to be a bartender in a Discotheque and Piano Bar in Ascona, the neighboring town to Brissago, where I worked the previous summer. How exciting! I love music and dancing, so I was especially looking forward to all the music and hopefully getting a dance or two in each shift.

My whole life in Europe was like this inner connection to the magic of serendipity, like an inner knowing that didn't get numbed out completely by the societal norms and fears that neutralize that connection in most of us. This inner knowing guided me to the right place and the right time where new possibilities opened up where prior to that there had seemed to be none. Again and again, when I reflect on the big picture of my life, it was, and is, like being on a magic-carpet ride. Sometimes though, when I either doubted or didn't listen to some of those intuitions, I stumbled into some very painful experiences. But in the end, even those were/are a part of the magic, because they taught me my blind spots, my fears, and my projections of self, reality and of others who weren't congruent with what was true and right in front of me and in me. We all learn through trial and error. There is no other way. I have learned that no matter what knowledge we carry, how educated we are, no matter what wise advice we have received via science or other bodies of wisdom, until we are put in a circumstance to test and put it in to action, we don't truly know anything. It's theory, borrowed knowledge,.It is not authentically ours. Experience is how and where we learn. This is the arena where we are challenged to put our knowing into practice, and often be stretched to go beyond what we think we know, to attain new wisdom and understanding. This is where utilizing knowledge can catalyze transformation in us, making the knowledge a part of who we are. The knowledge I now live by and share that has helped me create the fulfilling life I now have only came through trial and error. Through taking many risks and wrestling with the many contradictions and polarities I encountered in myself and in life, Through my experiences I now have a functional framework of observation and navigation that is effective and congruent in processing and sorting information. This enables me to utilize all experiences to grow and evolve in a balanced and harmonious way. Life is about growth and expansion, opening to new possibilities. When we open to life and step out of our comfort zone, this is where magic and serendipities are generated from.

Getting this job as a Bartender in Ascona was another incredible serendipitous energy flow that took place at the end of the last season just days before I was getting ready to leave the Hotel in Brissago. Magic truly does happen.

* * *

During the last summer in Brissago, almost every night, some of my colleagues and I would hitch a ride to Ascona to dance after work at the same club I was going to be working at, Il Pirate. That's when and where I met BJ the DJ. She was from England and played the most amazing mixes. I got to know her and asked her if she could make me some mixed tapes that I could buy from her. She was really happy and eager to do that. We became friends and met for coffee on the Piazza Grande at least once a week. The Piazza Grande was a strip along the waterfront on Lago Maggiore, full of restaurants, cafés and tourist shops with a breathtaking view of the lake and mountains.

Just before I was getting ready to leave for my trip home, BJ and I agreed to meet at the restaurant above the discotheque outside on the Terrace. I was waiting for her for about 40 minutes but she hadn't arrived. Just as I was taking the last sip of my cappuccino, getting ready to pay and leave, a waiter came up to me and asked me if I was waiting for BJ. I said yes. He told me she was inside; that she had a migraine and was waiting for me there; as she needed to stay out of the Sun. That made me happy to get to see her before I left.

When I went in, I found her sitting with an older gentleman. I naturally greeted BJ with one of my big hugs and sat down to join them. She introduced us.

His name was Carlo, he was the owner of the Disco, Piano Bar and the Restaurant that were all in the same building. He asked questions about me, where I came from, what I was doing in Tessin, so I shared about the hotel where I worked. I also shared that I wasn't happy there and that I was looking for a new job for the following season. He looked at me thoughtfully, smiled and right then and there he offered me a job. Wow! If BJ hadn't had a migraine and if I hadn't gone that day, which was the last day I had a chance to see BJ before she went back to England and I went back to Canada, that would not have happened. I could not have orchestrated this experience even if I tried. There is a subtle force governed by the Law of Magnetism/Attraction that is constantly at work in the background of our lives. Life is truly magical when we can tap in to those subtle flows, knowingly and even unknowingly, to follow those intuitive moments that are like a very subtle breeze, and let it do its magic. If I had followed my impatience while waiting for BJ, I would have totally missed out. But a feeling told me to stay and wait and be patient. The course of my entire life was changed that afternoon. Again.

When we learn to pay attention and master the ability to tap in to the greater fields of energy working with and through us, and we learn to know ourselves and the unique language of our body and soul, we open ourselves to the realms of magic and miracles, which are really just universal laws of cause and effect, resonance and magnetism. There are forces that govern all creation. Most often, though, we can get so caught up in our minds, stories, and interpretations of reality, that we don't connect authentically to the moment. When we are not fully present we are unable to catch those subtle clues that life, our Higher Self if you will, is nudging us toward.

* * *

While visiting Rhienhold before going back to Switzerland I spent a lot of time walking to my mountain. I also connected with some old childhood friends and had a good time. It was a nice interlude.

Prior to leaving Toronto I went to a metaphysical store and purchased many spiritual books, music, and lots of crystals, so I was enjoying having the time to read as well. That was my new fascination. I started reading one of the books when I was on my mountain that really moved me and awoke my spirit of adventure. It's called *Medicine Woman,* by Lynn Andrews. It's about one woman's journey into the mystical world of spirituality and shamanism who was an apprentice of two native women in the back bush of Alberta. My enthusiasm for learning and discovering more was growing and was insatiable. I was also getting so excited to get to Ascona and could hardly wait to catch the train there in a few days. An acquaintance Roland Koehler offered to pick me up at the train station and bring me to Ascona. He was also going to help me find an apartment. I was excited about that and already imagining the possibilities of what it would look like and how I would decorate it.

When I arrived at the bar in Ascona, I was given a room above the restaurant for the first month where I would live until I found my own place. I was really discovering myself, who I was and all I had lived already. I was beginning to look at my past and how varied were the different phases I had experienced until then

I had a picture book of many pictures from my life so I put them all up on the wall: my baby pictures, my pre-punk pictures, my punk pictures, the ones from when I was modeling before I went to Germany and the ones from my time when I was doing my practicum at the hotel in Germany and then the last place in Switzerland.

It was like a timeline mosaic I had created on my wall. Sometimes I would look at it and reflect on all the expressions and explorations of life and self I had already experienced. It was actually a bit mind-bending. By observing myself in that way it somehow opened my first deep awareness of the impermanence of life and identity. I had witnessed that in nature and knew it on some level, but this really sank in. I started seeing myself and my possibilities in a new light.

I would go into deep meditations with those reflections; they grounded me and strengthened my capacity to observe myself and life. When I looked at where I was from where I had been, it was a pretty incredible journey. I could never have imagined myself being where I was years before.

So I set up my room with many nature pictures too, and I put up a little altar with my crystals, smudge, and my beeswax candle that Gennie gave me, perched in the trifold goddess vase I had found in a shop on Queen street in Toronto before I left. I also had a bunch of the magazines from Andre that I was eager to read with all kinds of different articles on spirituality and all that stuff. On one of those magazines there was a picture on the cover of an angel that looked so beautiful. It really moved me to the point that I went out and bought sketch paper and sketch pencils. I just felt like I had to draw it even though I had avoided drawing since I was a little girl.

Being away from home, I was finally free to just explore every aspect of me, whereas at home I felt confined, limited, and trapped by the patterns of relating that had developed and how my family saw me and their expectations. One of the most common criticisms that came my way was that I was too philosophical and I changed my way of thinking too much. What was actually happening was that I was always evolving to new understandings. Still am, always will be. I have no interest in staying the same, so to speak. I was so happy I no longer had to hide this part of me. I was free!

I had a beautiful view and a little balcony from the room that I had above the restaurant, where I could just relax and watch Lago Maggiore, the mountains, the lake, the movements on The Piazza, and just reflect. I had landed in such a beautiful paradise, again, more beautiful than I could ever have imagined.

I surprised myself with the drawing. I got so pulled into it, it was like being in a trance. Though there were some little parts I couldn't quite get the same way the artist had done it, the image of the face and the arms extending to heaven and the energy streams coming into her head from the cosmos was really beautiful. When the picture was completed it became the centerpiece on my altar for many years to come. I had no idea I could actually draw, how exciting! So many new experiences.

This was also going to be the first time I would be a bartender, so I had to go through some training days before I actually started to work. Carlo had just leased the Disco to two brothers, Marco and Chicho. We had a lot of fun and good laughs together as they taught me how to mix the different cocktails and drinks. For the first few weeks I worked on the main bar with them until I got everything down, then I was given my own little bar at the back of the Disco right by the dance floor. Dancing was my first joy and passion in life. Perfect!

I really enjoyed being a bartender. I didn't drink much alcohol myself but it was sure fun watching other people get sloshed and having a good time. I met a lot of really nice people and we would sometimes hang out after our bar closed and go to another bar, La Stella, that was just down the street that was open until 6 or 7 a.m. Sometimes we even drove to the neighboring town, Locarno, to the bakery and got fresh croissants for breakfast. Mmmmm, they were so yummy!

As I was doing all these new things and getting adjusted to my new work environment my mother came to visit with Reinhold.

* * *

After my mother had left when I was 7, a way that I coped with the abandonment was I created a relationship in my mind with her that she was my best friend. I really wanted that to be true. I really loved her, and of course I know she loved me, but there were many dynamics and patterns that had created deep ruptures in our connection. There was a volatility to her that kept me on guard. She herself had so much unhealed trauma as well. But I hadn't come to fully understand that yet.

I wanted to be loved so badly by her that I would always just agree with everything she said or told me about my father or anybody else.

But evidence of my suppressed sadness and anger came up every time I would go visit her within the first two three days of being there. I would have an emotional meltdown freak-out of sorts where I would yell at her; for what, I don't really remember. All I know is that the lid would come off the pressure cooker inside me and I would explode. Because of the nature of her patterning, instead of acknowledging my distressed state and gently finding out what's wrong she would get angry with me and punish me. She would give me the silent treatment and tell me to stay in my room until I come down and apologize.

I didn't understand everything I was feeling; I just knew that I felt a strong sense of being upset. In the end I would always comply and apologize and then the rest of the visit would be harmonious and we would have some good times, but really there was emotional suppression happening in me. Again, I know she loved me, but her unresolved traumas caused her to act out in those abusive ways. As long as I didn't trigger her, we had many fun times, with many moments of connecting and loving as well.

* * *

I was now cultivating my own world views and my own way through life. I felt nervous and apprehensive about her upcoming visit. It had been quite a while since I had spent a lot of time with her on my own. I had grown and changed so much that I felt a little awkward being with her. We were sitting at a cafe at the Piazza Grande after having walked around the town for a little bit. At one point, a mature lady, perhaps in her 50s, walked by us, dressed very youthfully. My mother started criticizing her immediately. Normally I always went along with everything she said, but this time I couldn't. Since all of my new experiences were opening me up to my own thoughts and perceptions, I had to speak up.

"Maybe dressing that way makes her feel happy or is fulfilling some part of her," I said. "You can't just judge her like that."

She turned to look at me, with the most aggravated and stern expression, "Who do you think you are? You always think you know everything! How dare you talk to your mother this way!"

She got up and stormed back up to the room where she and Reinhold were staying above the restaurant. I was absolutely dumbfounded! What had just happened? All I did was make a comment, it wasn't an attack. My voice wasn't even raised. And I by all means have never felt that I know everything, so where was that coming from?

I finished my cappuccino and slowly walked back to my room. She ignored me the rest of the day.

We were supposed to go for dinner that night. I felt the tension and was nervous about receiving her wrath. When she got angry, man, she could turn somebody to stone and then shatter them.

Well I was right to be afraid. She laid into me at the restaurant table like never before. What an ungrateful daughter I was, how dare I speak to her as I did, I'm arrogant and also conceited, she said. "Look at all the pictures you have on your wall of you...." and blah blah blah blah. She went on this incredibly hurtful tirade for about 30 minutes. I had already gone numb after about 10 minutes. She got up and stormed out of the restaurant with Reinhold, who had just sat there looking at me with sympathy. My friend Gerald, who owned the restaurant where we were, brought me a cocktail while raising his eyebrows and giving me a compassionate look as well.

My body was shaking. The whole artificial world I had created around my relationship with my mother crumbled before my very eyes. I saw I was not allowed to be my own person, that if I didn't continue always agreeing with her, it seemed like there was no real foundation to our relationship. This was devastating, and brought up all the anger from all the years of her emotional manipulations and domination tactics that she used to keep me in line all my life.

I gratefully drank my cocktail and, stunned beyond belief, went back to my room and journaled the experience.

What would happen next? How would we move forward and bridge this experience? I didn't feel the need to apologize for anything. I didn't do anything except for the first time speak my true mind but even that I did very gently in a conversational manner, not a confrontational one. I decided I didn't care anymore. Anger is a good way to numb pain. I would not concede to her manipulating me anymore. "I would no longer be her puppet" were the words I wrote in my journal. That is how I felt in that moment.

The next morning I woke up to find her leaving five days earlier than planned, telling me I am not her daughter anymore, that she disowns me and wants nothing more to do with me. Wow! She sure had a temper. Now that I have come to know and understand her and her traumas better, it all makes sense that she was triggered and reacted that way. But at the time, it was really hurtful and confusing.

My imagined and glorified relationship had just gone up in smoke and I had no idea what actually connected us anymore. That really destabilized me in many ways that at the time I was not willing to acknowledge. I reacted defensively and just said to myself, "Okay fuck it," and let her go. Basically she had disowned me because I made a comment against what she thought I should have said in response. So I should have laughed and agreed and criticized this human being who I knew nothing about how or what had made her to be as she is. No way! That was far too far against the true grain of my heart.

I let her go out of my life. I let her have her last word and never made any comments as she walked out the door. Part of me actually felt relief, like I was freed. She no longer lived in Germany, so I knew I would not have to encounter her very often. I felt good that she would be that far away, but still, my heart broke under my bravado. I continued to go deeper and deeper into learning meditation as a way to process and to keep moving forward rather than getting stuck in those emotions.

One day shortly after all this happened I went walking through the Locarno market for the first time. I met a guy who had a booth selling jewelry and lots of crystals. His name was Serge. We hit it off great. I bought a beautiful amethyst ring, that I still have, and a few other pieces of jewelry that had crystals and gemstones in them. He told me about a metaphysical bookstore not far from where we were. That excited me to no end! You can guess what happened next....

I walked over there right away. Brigitte, the owner, greeted me warmly. It was a beautiful store. There were so many things I wanted to buy and read. I was in heaven! Every chance I got after that day I went to her store. It was called Andromeda after the celestial constellation. I learned many things about aromatherapy, energy healing, and crystals from Brigitte. Eventually she started inviting me to her meditation group once a week. We would meet in the lower floor of this beautiful old church that was perched on a cliff in the mountains with a stream running alongside it. In a way it was similar to the one I used to go to in Brissago only that one was an abandoned church. This one was still very much in use. It was so old that it felt like traveling back in time.

I was growing and learning so much. Brigitte made a comment about how deeply and fast I would go into meditation, that I needed to be careful that I don't go too deep, that I stay grounded and present here even as I'm in the meditation. It was true I could go off into the ethers very easily. When I think of it, that kind of dissociation, separating from reality, was part of my survival mechanism as a child, when I would just zone out at school and at home. This made sense as to why meditation came so easy to me.

*   *   *

A funny story relating to being in that state…When I used to do live modeling in front of stores and in in store windows, I would have to sit still for 20-25 minutes at a time with no blinking. Doing the meditations I was learning with Brigitte made me remember that feeling. I see now that I was already naturally meditating when doing that work. It was quite fun, and I enjoyed the challenge of being absolutely still. Sometimes a small group of people would gather around me trying to figure out if I was real or not. One time a little child came to walk around me, touched me, and I twitched. The poor little guy screamed, dropping his glass juice jar and cried while everybody else who had been standing around waiting to figure out if I was real, just laughed their heads off. It was truly funny. I laughed with them.

* * *

I spent more and more time with Brigitte in the store, taking in as much as I could. I had bought many meditation tapes from different approaches, and just enjoyed being there. I met a lot of interesting people, too. I was grateful to have this sanctuary to go to whenever I wanted to be with likeminded people on the path to self-awareness.

One day when I had some time off I went to Heidelberg for three days to visit an old friend I had worked with during my practicum. He had actually been my first boyfriend but we were still really good friends.

While he worked during the day I explored the town. I met another guy on the street market that made and sold really neat crystal jewelry with this kind of clay stuff that dried as solid as plastic that you could form any way you were inspired to. Victor was his name. We chatted for a while and I bought a few crystals from him. I told him where I worked in Ascona if he ever made it down that way to stop by and say hi.

He ended up visiting the next week. I asked him to teach me how to make that jewelry and he said sure. It was so great working in a bar because I had the daytime free to do whatever I wanted. He taught me while we hung out at the beach and then I bought a bunch of supplies from him, almost everything he had, actually. He was going back to India in two weeks, so it helped him both to offload and have money for his trip. What a serendipity that it worked out so well for both of us!

By that time I had moved into my new apartment. Just next door was a lumber store so I walked over and bought supplies to make a wooden jewelry showcase like the one Victor had. I wanted to make and sell jewelry on the markets too, for fun. The case turned out so beautiful. I amazed myself again, having never built anything like that before. I met so many other people at the markets who were on a similar wavelength. I had no idea that there were so many people into what I was into, I was so happy. I was also learning Tai Chi with another woman I had met at a cafe one day. Another interesting person was a painter named Rolando who made the most mystical images I had ever seen. I met a psychic, too. I was in heaven, like a child in a candy store again is how I felt. Like I had felt at the world healing meditation.

We all have different callings in life. When we find connections that feed that innate way of being, where we fit in and belong, it's incredibly profound, empowering and grounding.

As I grew closer with these people I became less close with the ones I worked with. I now found them really shallow. They started thinking I was turning a bit weird because I was changing. In fact, I was seeing through their dysfunctions and masks behind their personas of alcohol and drugs. I didn't want to judge them, I just didn't feel comfortable with them anymore.

One night at work this guy came into my area of the bar by the dance floor. When I saw him I felt electricity shoot through me. *Whoa! what was that?* I thought. Yes, he was really cute but I've seen many good-looking men and that never happened.

He had longish blond wavy hair, and was wearing a cotton shirt, jeans, and moccasins. My heart literally skipped a beat when I saw the moccasins. Why? I assumed it's because I felt such a strong connection to Native Americans the more I read about their way of being and their understanding of life and spirituality. I couldn't keep my eyes off him. I wanted to know him. I had never been taken with someone like that before.

At one point he was standing at the side of the dance floor. I decided to go clear some dirty glasses that were on the floor near him. I passed him and reached down to get the glasses. When I stood up he was right beside me. I said hi; he nodded, and for some reason lightly touched my shoulder. Again I felt a rush of energy. What was this? I had been reading all about past lives and stuff so I thought maybe we knew each other in a past life. Maybe we were Native Americans together. Who knows? After bringing the glasses back to my bar I turned around to look at him again, but he was gone.

Every night after that I kept an eye out for him but he never returned.

I kept busy. I was having fun making my jewelry during the day, going to the beach, enjoying my cappuccinos on the Piazza Grande and meeting friends for deep conversations about reality and truth. One of my favorite things was visiting an old church that is in the town center. I love old churches, always have. I was happy in my world and eventually stopped thinking of him.

A few weeks later after work I went to La Stella, the all night bar down the road from where I worked, again. They had a bar area out front;to the back it was like a big gymnasium, lots of space to dance. I so loved to dance. I had studied jazz and ballet for six years as a child until I was 13. Dancing opened a portal of freedom for me to express through movement. I was a wild, free dancer for sure, still am actually!

I went in to the bar area first to say hi to my bartender friend Pierre. He was an older gentleman who took me out for tea a few times. We were catching up with each other a bit in between his serving drinks. He was a kind man, very joyful and positive. When I turned around to look around the bar, there he was, the moccasin man, sitting at the opposite bar, looking right at me. I got goosebumps and my stomach turned into butterflies. Our eyes met, it felt very intense. I said "Ciao"' and he said "Ciao" back. I was nervous, so I looked away.

I didn't know what else to do so I went to the dance area to dance my bootie off. I think dancing was my first language! I love it so much. At the end of the night, well really, at the beginning of morning, I walked out to say goodbye to Pierre. He, moccasin man, was still there, this time on the same side of the bar as I had to walk by to exit. I said "hi" again and he asked "Do I know you?" I felt like saying, ya, from many past lives ago! I chuckled to myself and then said no, not really, that we had seen each other a few weeks before at Il Pirata where I worked. He thought back for a moment then nodded his head in recognition. He asked me where I was from. A big smile formed on his face when he heard I was from Canada. He said he always has wanted to go to Canada.

His name was Emanuele, he was from the neighboring town of Locarno where I had met Serge and where Brigitte's shop was. *Nice,* I thought. My heart was beating so fast it's not funny, or perhaps it is. Who was this guy and why did he have that effect on me? We exchanged a few more words, said good-bye and then I left to go back to work to pick up my bicycle.

Normally I rode along the lake on Piazza Grande but I felt an inner nudge -- me and my nudges -- to ride a different route, so I did. Guess who I ended up riding past? Yep, there he was, walking down the street. I called to him and wished him a good day, as it was about 6:30 in the morning. He did the same but then said something I didn't understand so I circled around back to him. I ended up getting off my bike and walked with him. He had to pass where I lived on his way back home. What a coincidence!

We immediately started talking about spirituality, Native American teachings, life etc. -- all the stuff I love exploring and talking about. He even wore a turquoise necklace, he said, for protection. How amazing was this? I had met a guy who is actually interested in all of this stuff! Wow! I was in love! It's so sweet when I remember the inner innocence and newness of that time in my life. It felt like spring to my soul, with all these incredible new flowers and beautiful creations coming forth that I had no idea were planted in my inner earth.

* * *

Moving to Europe was one of the best things that ever happened to me. It helped me to birth my soul in ways that I couldn't have back home in Ontario. Even though there were many traumas that took place in Europe as well in the years to come, each experience enriched me, gave me something that helped me heal my childhood traumas and grow into the woman I am now.

Sometimes blessings and miracles are recognized in hindsight. It doesn't remove the experience of pain and trauma that I had to work through still, but it can help the trauma to be resolved and healed. We need to develop a vastness in our perceptions and awareness to leave enough room for the possibility that no matter how terrible or painful an experience is, somewhere there is something good that can come out of it. At the very least, I can choose to create something good out of it.

* * *

We continued walking until we came to my home. I asked him if he might like to come in for a coffee or tea. He said yes, he would like that. When we entered my apartment he immediately started looking around at all my crystals, my books, incense, and the posters of the mystical paintings I had from the artist Rolando that I mentioned earlier. He started to cry.

I went to him and asked him what was happening. He was sobbing so deeply. I put my arm around his shoulder and as I did this he said that everything in my home reminded him of the spirituality he had felt and experienced in the past, but that he now felt lost and disconnected from. He shared that in Columbia South America, somebody did some dark magic on him. Ever since then he's been lost and in the dark. He said it was so beautiful being in my place and so healing. I didn't really know what to say except that he's safe and that he can heal and reclaim that part of him. He shared a little more about his life and I about mine as we drank our coffee, and then he went on his way.

He told me where he worked as a lifeguard at the public beach and pool and said that I should pop by sometime and say hi. As he was about to leave, he reached in his pocket and pulled out a little brown-glass bottle and gave it to me. He said it was Sandalwood oil that he had brought back from India on one of his many trips there. I love Sandalwood, it's one of my favorite oils. I thanked him, and we did the traditional kissing on each cheek as is done over there.

I was over the moon happy. If I hadn't changed my bike route that evening none of that magic would have happened. I was in awe of life and curious of what might come.

It was several days after that meeting that I built up the courage to go see him at the pool.

I went through the turnstile, paid my fee, and just as I was walking through, there he was. My whole body started to shake, I wasn't sure what to say or what to do, but there I was. He came to me and said, "I am happy beyond words for your visit." My heart melted. Nobody had ever said anything like that to me before.

We ended up having the most amazing romance all summer long. We did meditations together, we studied crystals together and spent so much beautiful time in Nature. It was just so easy to get along with each other. I was so happy. The only thing that was challenging for me at times is that he lived in his own bubble where he didn't have much sense of time. So sometimes he would come really late and often there could be two or three days that I wouldn't hear from him. That was normal for him; that was his rhythm. Knowing that was a part of the uniqueness and beauty of him, I did my best to find my way with that. But for me it activated emotional triggers of abandonment. Of course the more you feel you have gained, the more the fear can creep in of losing it all.

He had a friend named Bibi who was a clairvoyant and whom we often spent time with. She said that we had actually had many past lives together and that's why we felt such a strong connection. That felt right for me, it was the only explanation to why I felt so strongly when we met. Being with him opened my heart in a space and place that I don't think had been open since all the trauma when I was seven. I just felt so at home with him and he felt that with me as well.

There was one small difference though, he was afraid of being in a relationship after his heart was broken by his previous girlfriend. Whereas I was gung-ho ready and willing.

One thing we spent a lot of time doing was leather and bead work projects. I think the last time I had ever worked with leather in any way was in Brownies and Girl Guides. He had a lot of leather and beads he had purchased in Indonesia his last trip. I watched him make his things with ease while I struggled trying to make mine absolutely perfect, and then I would get frustrated when I couldn't. Somehow my doing this with him brought to the surface the part of me that had shut down with the belief that I wasn't good at anything creative, and if I was to make something it had to be perfect, whatever perfect was to me. It was really quite interesting watching myself and feeling how uptight my body would get if I felt I had made a mistake. At one point I threw a bracelet across the room in frustration. I can't help but chuckle when I remember that now. But, then I picked it back up and through watching him and his ease I started learning to be more at ease myself, having patience and being okay with flaws. That was very new for me. More healing and more growth, how wonderful!

He was always talking about his trips to Asia and that he was going to be going to the Philippines again that winter. But first he was going to Thailand and he asked me if I wanted to meet him in there. I said yeah, for sure, that would be amazing. So we created a new project with the leather and started making our own travel bags. It was an amazing process. I made this beautiful backpack with a burnt image on the front from a postcard I had found at Brigitte's store. It was a picture of the earth embraced by the roots of a large tree that extended up and turned into a man and a woman with branches extending into the universe. I love that image depicting our connection with Nature and our stewardship of taking care of Mother Earth. Doing the leather and bead work became a new meditation for me. My old core patterns were transforming into new healthier ways of being and perceiving.

Work at the Disco was the same as always, but I was becoming more distant with my bosses and the people I worked with. I was looking forward to the end of the season, I didn't really enjoy being there so much anymore.

Two weeks before the end of the season Emanuele invited me to go on a camping trip into the mountains. I had never gone camping before and was a little bit nervous but of course said yes. We were gone for about five days. Every night we camped at a new place, climbing the mountain. It was so beautiful, like nothing I'd ever seen or experienced before. One morning while I was bathing in the very cold mountain stream a beautiful little fox came for his morning bath and drink. I was behind a rock so he didn't see me so I was able to watch him. He was so beautiful. On our last night we stopped at a little chalet at the peak of the mountain that served warm meals and drink. We had soup, homemade bread, and fresh mountain cheese. It was the most amazing cheese I had ever eaten. Then we made our way back to set up our tent for our last night.

I remember feeling very uneasy. Emanuele was really silent and to me silence always indicated I was in trouble or something was wrong, based on the silent treatments I used to get from my mother. My insecurities about having done something wrong were surfacing. For me doing something wrong meant I would be abandoned. This was one of my subconscious beliefs that had developed when my mom left, and also through the loss of my sister. I was always afraid of being abandoned and rejected.

That was my Achilles heel. I felt such a tightness in my gut that night, which of course created a strain on our otherwise comfort with each other.

It doesn't take much on the subtle realms to affect a connection. As soon as something is withheld, a subtle tension develops, and the longer it remains either unresolved or hidden, it grows, collects more emotional stuff, like dust and creates big dust bunnies in our psyche. I didn't sleep well that night and woke up feeling very vulnerable. We made our way down the mountain and stopped to have a little bite to eat halfway down from the remainder of our food. He was really silent still and I think he was feeling my subconscious tension, which was making things worse.

When we got down to the little village we stopped in a bakery to grab some sweets and snacks. I went into the washroom and started crying. My inner fears were taking over and I really needed to shift my focus because I didn't want to put the pressure on him that would create more pressure by asking him if something was wrong. So I dried my tears and went back out and pretended like nothing had happened and tried to smile and have a conversation with the person behind the counter, making some jokes so that I could laugh. We then pressed on down to the bottom and arrived at his car. He drove me home pretty much in silence, we hugged and gave each other a kiss good-bye. I still felt distant from him. When I got into my apartment I just broke down and cried. I didn't really even understand why I was crying so much; it was much deeper than any real circumstance that was happening. I just let myself feel it and let it flow through.

I didn't hear from him for five days. Those five days my neuroses really went crazy. I did my best to journal to express as much as I could to free my mind. I did all my crystal healing meditations. I went to see Brigitte and got some advice from her. But inside I just felt so vulnerable and so afraid that I had done something wrong that his love would be removed from me.

When he finally came by I looked a mess, I said I had been sick with a cold or something. This activated his caring and he took care of me, made me soup and went to the store and got me some things and he became more affectionate again. That settled my heart.

A few days later after he had come to see me I had to move out of my apartment. He came to help me out and we moved all of my things into his parent's basement storage space. I was going to stay with him and his family until I flew to Thailand. He was going to be flying in just a few days. It was November so my season contract at the disco was over. I felt so nervous about him going and us not being together for a few weeks. *What if he meets somebody new that he likes more than me?* I had so many insecurities. I was so afraid all the time of being left behind. I experienced this even with just friends, not only with him.

Before he left we each finished the bracelets we had made for each other that had both of our hair entwined and braided together. We said we would exchange them in Thailand. No matter the expressions of love he gave me, it was never enough for me to feel safe. I observed that with greater awareness for the first time in my life. I was becoming aware that I really needed healing in that regard. I spoke with Brigitte about it too; she was always supportive and encouraging me to meditate and keep reading books that can help me understand myself better. When he left, I spent lots of time finishing my backpack in his room, hoping to be done in time for my departure while listening to Cat Stevens and John Denver over and over again. I loved them!

Nothing else of great significance happened in those two weeks except my mother called me because she was afraid I might die in Thailand. I said if I die, I die; it's a part of life,

I'll die living. I was just sharing how I saw it but she took it as me being sassy back to her. Well, my heart had shut down toward her anyway so I just ignored her comments and said good-bye.

I spent some more time with Bibi and Brigitte before the final days of preparing to leave. I also bought my first set of Tarot cards and was excited to bring them with me and learn about them while I was away.

Off to another adventure! I could hardly wait.

3

AN ADVENTURE OF
A LIFETIME BEGINS

I walk alone, along the corridor, I'm not sure what I feel.
I'm on my way somewhere, To some forgotten place,
A place I know exists.
There's white light all around me,
Filling the hall and my being, showing me the clear path ahead.
I feel solid and sure.
Now there are arms reaching to me from behind the walls,
Beckoning me to come,
In such a gentle and peaceful way as if they mean well.
So, I pause and wonder for a moment, Should I go there?
In this moment I am thrust into a pool of confusion,
Where I lose all sense of reality…
Where I lose myself.
These hands that have lured me off my path.
They've tempted me with their apparent kindness and wisdom.
They've made me think twice about my own thoughts, testing
my solidity, making me doubt myself,
Creating illusions for me to follow.
Now, I try to find my way back.
- Journal Entry May 1991. Bonndorf Germany, 20 years of age.

The day came for my departure. Emanuele's father drove me to the train station at five in the morning so I could catch the train to Zurich, where I was catching my plane. It was going to be a total of 21 hours of flight plus a nine-hour stopover in Bucharest, Romania. What a long trip!

I slept most of the way to Romania; it was a smooth flight. When we landed in Bucharest it was so cold and the airport was made out of glass walls with no heating inside. Oh, my gosh, and now I had wait here for nine hours in the freezing cold? Yikes.

I passed through customs and went to the waiting area for my flight. I looked around and I was the only Caucasian person in the waiting area. Everyone in the waiting area were Thai and other Asian Descents. I had never experienced that before. It stirred up a lot of guilt and questions in me. In that space in that moment I was a minority.

I found a place to sit and felt really awkward and wondered if they all hated me because I am white, thinking of all the terrible things my white ancestors have done to ethnic races throughout history. It made me shudder at the thought of all that brutal violence. I remembered watching the movie *Dances with Wolves* with Emanuele just the month before and how my heart broke and felt broken for days after witnessing the genocide. I had only a little idea until then the extent of atrocities that had happened to the Native American People. The way our history books in school relay events I realized was very far from the facts. All these thoughts raced through me in those few moments.

All through school the kids that were nicest to me were kids from various ethnic backgrounds, so for me I really loved and appreciated them. I never thought of them as minorities or 'other' so I never imagined how they may have felt. With this new experience I got a glimpse of what it might have felt like to be them, and I felt so bad I had not realized it before.

It was a daunting and unsettling sensation. I felt disoriented and not quite sure how to be. I then took out my journal to redirect me and wrote about what I was experiencing and feeling.

A few moments later I looked up from my journal and saw these two lovely Thai women looking at me. They sent me big smiles, the tension dissolved from my body instantly. They invited me to come sit with them, so I did. They spoke broken English, but between that and physical gestures we connected nicely. They were so sweet and kind. We became instant friends.

A bit later some other western travelers came into the area. One guy sat close to us with his friends and pulled out a bottle of red wine. We all ended up sitting in a circle together, joking, laughing, and drinking wine. He and his friends had two more bottles, so we all got a bit drunk. Those nine hours thankfully went by fast because of that. We were all huddled on the ground in a circle in our sleeping bags trying to keep warm. It was a lot of fun.

Then we heard the call for our flight. We clumsily, in our somewhat drunken state, got up and made our way to the gate. Sasha, the guy who had the first bottle of wine, was totally sloshed; he could barely walk. We held him up and got him to his seat. It was hilarious!

It turned out me and the two Thai ladies, Mai and Pat, were sitting together in the emergency seating. Doubly nice, lots of space for my long legs, and I got to sit with these lovely women. Sasha sat in the row behind us.

The plane was so old and beaten down. The food trays had been ripped off and put in the pockets on the back seats where the magazines usually go. Mai's seat was loose and unstable and the material covering the seats was torn in many places. We looked at each other with big eyes. Oh my God. I hope we make it! Sasha just passed out with his feet in the aisle. During the flight the stewardess kept running over his feet hoping to wake him but it didn't work. We laughed a lot.

He was lucky he passed out because the flight was absolutely terrifying! There was turbulence like I had never experienced before, as in one of those thriller movies where the plane goes out of control. I got lifted out of my seat so many times. Mai and Pat pulled out their prayer beads and were praying almost the whole time. Me, I pulled out my pendulum, and prayed as well. I even went to the bathroom and asked if we will make it to Thailand alive. It was so scary. I got a yes. So I sure hoped it was accurate.

When we finally landed we were very late, so I got concerned that Emanuele might leave thinking I didn't come. I had a picture of him in my money belt so I gave it to Mai and asked her to look for him since she will be getting through customs much faster. She said she would. I just had a feeling he might leave before I got through, knowing him, and I had no way of knowing where to find him if he wasn't there. That was a very scary thought.

Turns out it was a good idea that I did that. Thank God/dess for my inner nudges! Emanuele told me later that he was just getting ready to leave because he already had been there for two hours when Mai approached him with her cart, looked at the picture I gave her, then showed it to him. "Is this you?' she asked. He said yes, so she told him to wait, I would be coming out soon. Phew. Thank God/dess again!

I came out and we had a really nice moment greeting each other. He took me to get a taxi to wherever it was we were going to be staying. It was incredible, all the people, the smells, the noise, again, like nothing I had ever experienced before. My senses were overloaded with wonder and awe! My energy was a bit frenetic though, nervous and anxious. No wonder after my flight experience, but also all the newness, as wonderful as it was, was also overwhelming. I laid my head on his lap in the back of the taxi and tried to relax.

It was a long drive to where we were staying in Bangkok. What a big city! We got out on this side road at a place called Guest House 59. It was a very old and run-down building.

There were a lot of travelers hanging out in the check-in area. He brought us to our room, it was a very new experience indeed. It was a simple space with one big bed and nothing else. Ripped curtains and screens with holes in them and lots of noise coming through the windows. Very different from anywhere I had been, that's for sure.

It was soooo hot, I needed to shower and change. We had a little nap and he took me for dinner at a street restaurant on Koh San Road. I was amazed at how many people there were. It was very exciting. All the street vendors were selling silk tops, music tapes from the 70's, jewelry, and stuff. I loved it. What an adventure.

The food was delicious, though I gave him my cilantro. There was so much on the top of my dish that when I bit into it, it was way too strong of a foreign flavor for me.

In Switzerland we had had our rhythm, but here everything, including Emanuele, felt so different. I was trying to feel out who I am, who we are together in this new environment. I felt a bit insecure, too. He said he had planned a trip for us to go to an island called Koh Phangan in a few days. That's exciting I thought, it made me happy that he did that. *So he does still love me*, I thought in the back of my mind.

On our way back to the guest house I bought a few sarongs and new tops that were more appropriate for the weather than what I had brought. On the way back to the Guest House he stopped to meet a guy where he bought some pot. I had only tried it once with him in Locarno and I had a mellow and happy experience, so I thought sure, that might help my nerves to relax a bit more. We went back to our room and he made a joint and lit it. He took a few tokes and then offered it to me. I didn't take much, but it was really strong.

I was expecting to have that nice mellow feeling again but instead I had an out-of-body experience that terrified me. That's the best way I can describe it. It felt like my soul left my body and I felt the sensation like in thriller movies when someone's in a hallway and no matter how fast they are trying to run, the hallway keeps lengthening leaving them unable to reach the door they were trying to get to. It was a freaky sensation I did not want to experience again. I spent that night in a state of angst and paranoia. I didn't let on to Emanuele what happened, lest he like me less, so silly, but that's how it was for me, so afraid of not being good enough that I could be rejected.

I was happy to preoccupy myself with jewelry-making the next day, it helped me direct and focus my scrambled mind. He had bought some new leather and beads for us to work with. He also introduced me to this Thai man named Chad who made moccasins, like the ones he was wearing when we met, and he made all kinds of Native American-styled beadwork and jewelry as well. Emanuele asked Chad to teach us how to create and bead from a bead loom. He was happy to do that. It was quite cool how he told us to make the loom. He said to buy two hair combs with small teeth, then get a piece of wood the length we wanted our bead piece to be and nail the combs on both ends and voila, we had our bead loom! '*Pretty ingenious*', I thought. I also bought myself a pair of moccasins. They were so comfortable.

We spent the afternoon learning to work the bead looms. I still felt a bit off but having that focus helped me orientate myself again. He took me to a temple with a large Buddha that was so beautiful. We ate at another street restaurant, so yummy; I discovered the Cashew Chicken dish, and all in all had a good day. But he still felt a bit distant, so my neurosis started re-emerging again.

That night when we got back to our guest house his ex-girlfriend showed up unexpectedly, the one who had broken his heart, and not by coincidence: she knew where he was and knew he was with me.

She had tried to make contact with him that summer when she found out he had a new girlfriend but he didn't respond to her. Emanuele's best friend Bibi had told me all about her and how she might try to win him over because she couldn't stand that he is with someone else, even though she was the one who had broken their relationship off years before. He had no idea she was going to be there and was just as surprised. He introduced us; I was friendly, but held myself back.

More neuroses surfaced in me. She was pretty and had travelled many places with him before. They had a lot of history together. I hoped that was the last time we would see her since we were leaving the following day.

The next day we were getting things together for going to catch the train to go to the island Koh Pha-ngan late that night. I fabricated a sickness. I convinced myself that I had something wrong with me and went to the doctor to get some medicine. This is what my insecurities drove me to do.

Last time when I was sick he showed great care. This time not so much. He seemed more irritated.

Nicole, his ex-girlfriend, came around again all smiley and flirty. She seemed like a nice girl. Under other circumstances I might have even liked her. However, I didn't like that she was there, nor what I could see she was up to. I just observed and did my best to keep my neuroses under cover. Not an easy task at all!

Fortunately, we were catching the train to the island that night. Emanuele was a little bit edgy and distant some moments; at others he was affectionate, it was really hard for me to read him.

It was a twelve-hour train ride. We did some leather and beadwork on the looms we had created but didn't talk much. The looms worked really well and I was happy to have something to do to distract me from my neurotic thinking that was starting to take over like a wildfire. Then we went to sleep until we woke up at our stop in Surat Thani.

We were picked up by an affiliate travel agency to the one with whom we booked the trip. We were then brought to their agency to wait until it was time to catch the ferry, at which time they would take us there. We drank some Thai iced tea and waited, also very yummy. My fears were still knowing at me and increasing by the minute. He felt so distant.

The ferry ride was beautiful. Being on the water soothed me deeply. I had only ever been on one other ferry before, in the North Sea in Germany when my mom, Rhienhold, and I visited some of his relatives there.

This, however, was a tropical paradise. Breathtaking! The awe in me grew and distracted me from my minds workings.

After about one hour we arrived to Tongsala, the port on Koh Pahngan. I felt like I had landed on Gilligan's Island! It wasn't developed at all. Just a few shops and restaurants made out of plywood and scrap wood, and only dirt roads. I loved it! We stopped at one of the restaurants to grab a bite to eat and ran into a friend of Emanuele's from home; Reto was his name. He was with his girlfriend. We sat with them and Reto suggested we go to the bungalow where they were staying, it was called the Seaview Rainbow. We said sure, as we hadn't yet decided where we were going to go yet anyway.

The parking lot was filled with trucks that would take people to the various bungalows around the island. We jumped into the one for Seaview Rainbow and headed off. The roads were rough, big potholes every few feet, surrounded by tall coconut trees. I was ecstatic for the beauty I was seeing. Especially after being in Bangkok where there is virtually no Nature within the city.

I felt like a little girl going to Disney Land. We drove for quite a while and then finally arrived at this beautiful beachfront bungalow rental place. Wow! We rented one that was semi-close to the beach and settled in. Emanuele started drinking a lot, and smoking a lot of pot, which I no longer took part in since my last experience in Bangkok that first night. He grew distant by the day. It was as if I didn't exist. I found myself wanting to pretend I was sick again when, in those moments, I finally consciously woke up to what I was doing. It had been such a natural function for me, feel insecure, then get sick. I started journaling about this observation and asked myself, "Why do I do this?"

I reflected back on my life and was brought back to the time of my sister's accident. I had lost my sense of place and family structure. At the age I was when all this happened, I read somewhere that our family is our identity until we start to individuate at nine years of age. That made sense when I reflected on it. Mine was completely shattered. I hardly saw my parents in that time because my dad had to work and then he would go to the hospital, my mom lived in the city and was at the hospital with Lorri all the time, while I was always shuffled back and forth from different people's homes, as mentioned earlier.

I saw the equation my little mind created back then … Sickness=Attention=proof of being loved. I made myself sick all the time when I was little. Sometimes I was really sick, but the majority of the time I faked it, looking to receive love and attention. Wow! What a discovery of self-awareness that was for me; to admit it to myself was incredible. I was amazed how I could have had that pattern all my life and been blind to it. I wondered what else I had been blind to that I had yet to discover.

That day, I made a vow to myself that even if I was sick, I wouldn't ask for help. I needed to break that pattern. That's what I did. Years later I found a balance with that, but the first few years I was committed to that vow and it did help me to be more self-reliant and break the victim mentality pattern that was at the root of that pattern.

Since Emanuele and I had always connected by sharing thoughts and observations, I was excited to share this discovery with him, thinking that maybe it may catalyze a remembrance in him of who we were together. His response was very bland and completely disinterested. That hurt me deeply. He was very different from how he used to be with me, like he was a different person all together.

I was so happy to have uncovered this hidden pattern, and had hoped to share that joy with him. In that moment I could see my once-best friend and lover and I were clearly growing apart. No longer having the pattern of pretending to be sick to numb the reality, I now had to meet it. It was very new and painful for me to find my way through my insecurities and fears. But my awareness grew immensely because of that experience. It was like it opened the bottleneck in my soul/consciousness, that had been blocked for so long. Now new energy, insight and awareness could move me into new ways of knowing myself and life that before that moment could not because of the block of my emotional pain pattern. I just focused on my bead work. We exchanged some moments at mealtime but there was no real connecting.

A few days later he casually shared an idea he had to create a signpost with the names of different countries on it, with their distance in miles pointing in the direction of the country, to put on the beach. That sounded like a fun idea that we might reconnect through. I, the eternal optimist, told him I thought it was a great idea. He asked Oi, the owner, if he would like to have a sign like that on his property. He said he would love it.

Here was a project I hoped might rekindle our connection again since being creative together is how we bonded before. Oi helped us get the supplies we needed and we got to work. I had so much fun exploring my creativity through painting. I painted the eyes of the Buddha for the sign to Kathmandu, and a few others, but that was my masterpiece. My insecurities around painting were diminishing rapidly.

We worked on the sign for a few weeks, everyday together. While we were painting everything seemed okay, but at night he changed, he would become distant again. I did my best to not question him, thinking that might push him away more, and just give him space to sort out whatever was going on inside him.

There were moments it felt like we had connected a bit again through this shared project, but the more he drank and smoked pot, the more distant he became, until he wouldn't even say good-night to me anymore and in the mornings would just get up and go without a word. It was like I stopped existing in his world. It was absolute torture. We had been so close. I didn't know what to do. I didn't want to let go but was starting to realize I might have to if he didn't communicate with me to get through this. There is only so much space we can give to someone when in a situation like this. There comes a point where we need to take care of ourselves first and foremost rather than trying to take care of them and their feelings. I was approaching that point.

Once Emanuele and I went for a long walk to a place called Haadrin Beach, it took about 2 hours. It was a beautiful walk along the shoreline. We didn't talk much, just walked in silence. On the way, guess who we bumped into walking towards us? Nicole, his ex. They chatted and as they did I noticed that Emanuele got an erection, showing very clearly through his sarong. My heart dropped. I pretended I didn't see it and just kept walking. We had lunch in Haadrin, I bought some nice sarongs, tried to get his attention, to look sexy, but he was gone, I could feel it. My heart was racing as I realized there was likely no chance of us reconnecting.

One day a new group of people came to stay at Seaview that offered me some reprieve from what I was going through with him. Bashka, Loreene, Vincent, and a Sadhu from India.

Loreene was actually renting the house across the street and offering massage and yoga classes. I ended up spending a lot of time with them. Particularly with Loreene, as she was from Germany. I felt really seen by all them. Spending time with them fed my heart well. I had been starting to lose sense of who I was with all this happening with Emanuele. He had been my mirror of me until all this started.

Now, I would eat all my meals with my new friends, and he did his own thing. They all appreciated me and were amazed at my insights on life and healing, being only 20 years old. Bashka said I must be an old soul to be so engaged with all this stuff from a young age. That made me feel good. When I had shared about the self- blessing ritual I practiced through my teen years she was blown away. I received their admiration gratefully. I felt like a plant and their acknowledgements were like water and sunlight, encouraging me to grow. We all need to feel seen and be valued for who we are and the uniqueness we bring into the world. It was a true Godsend that they were there. Loreene also taught meditation and movement therapy. I joined her every day to learn all I could from her. She was an amazing woman.

There was this one stretch that she taught me that made me almost pass out, because it increased circulation through my neck to my brain so much. It felt like it unlocked an energetic block that had been there for a long time. I felt a rush of energy flush through my body when I did it and got really dizzy for a moment.

I really liked Yoga, it felt good for my body and mind. Some days we did expressive-movement classes, which I loved, and always we shared a meal that she would prepare afterwards.

We would talk about everything. She inspired me so much. What a strong and empowered woman to have as a mentor. She also spoke really good Thai. She had been married to a Thai man for several years, and had lived in Thailand already for 14 years. Amazing! Such a strong and self- made woman.

I am so grateful for her presence there. I am not sure how I would have navigated the situation without her. She also taught me the basics of Thai massage.

Massage was something that always came natural to me. When I was 10 I used to get massages for my asthma from a neighbor of my grandma. She would teach me her techniques, too, as she worked on me. It really helped my lungs. I loved giving massages. At family gatherings I would get paid a quarter for a shoulder rub. It was nice learning some new techniques from Loreene and it opened me to want to learn more about healing.

In that time another girl from Canada, named Stacey, came to Seaview. We became instant friends. When I shared with her my situation with Emanuele, she sympathized with me and said it must be even harder because it's happening in a foreign country with no family or friends around. I agreed it was. I hadn't quite thought of it that way, and that made me even more grateful for Loreene. It was all getting to the point that I decided, with the encouragement of Stacy, that I would be fine to leave Seaview and go on travelling by myself. There was a place I had seen, that looked beautiful, when Emanuele and I were at Hadrin Beach, so I decided I would go there. There were lots of travelers and they had a full-moon party coming up. Loreene also supported my decision so I told him I was going.

It had the effect of an ice cold shower on him.

He knew how terrified I had been to travel there by myself. Being a young, single woman in countries like Thailand isn't all that safe. He was clearly shocked and concerned. I just said I can't do this anymore.

"You used to be my best friend," I said, "and we had always promised each other that even if the romance faded we would keep our friendship, but you aren't even that anymore and it breaks my heart, but I have to take care of myself and leaving is the only way I can do that right now. It's far too painful staying."

He burst into tears, buckled to his knees and said he didn't know what was going on with him. That it's not my fault, he's sorry, that he does love me. I thanked him for that but said I still have to go, I needed to heal the hurt this had caused in me. I told him I loved him too, but that we clearly need some space between us to see where we go from there, if anywhere at all.

He got up and went to his bag and pulled out the bracelet with our hair that he had made for me, and asked if we could exchange them now before I go so he can also have the one I made for him, too. I said sure. We spoke a blessing prayer for each other and exchanged them. I was set to leave the next morning. For the first time in so long, he reached for my hand and said good-night to me when we went to bed. I cried and fell asleep.

The next morning I arose early to get in the truck going back to Tongsala. We hugged, saying good-bye. At least I could feel some warmth again from his heart and between us, but still I knew I had to go if anything was going to change. From Tongsala, I caught a water taxi that took me to Haadrin.

On the way there I was enjoying the view of the beautiful turquoise waters and green palm trees, then all of a sudden a flying fish jumped over the boat and slapped me in the face. Yes! I am beginning to wake up, thank you very much! I chuckled to myself.

When I got there I found a great place on a cliff called Serenity Bungalows. That place became my sanctuary. I set up my altar of crystals and sacred prayer items like I always did wherever I went, then climbed down the cliff to have lunch. All the restaurants had T.V's where they played movies most of the day, so I had lunch and watched a movie. It was a great change and distraction for me to do that. I started relaxing.

Later on that day I went swimming. The water was more wild on that beach compared to where we had been. It was windy and the waves were quite large. I went in anyway, with the surf crashing strong and loud against my body. *What force, what beauty*, I thought. While I was in the water I did an experiment. I was always holding my body rigid, bracing for the impact of the waves. I found myself wondering what would happen if I let go of my rigidity and just went with the wave. So I tried it. Wow! *What an insight,* I thought. My awareness awoke and expanded to a new way seeing and perceiving life.

Metaphorically, I thought to myself, waves can be like the circumstances that sometimes come at us so hard that we often fight or resist them. But, if we can learn to flow with them, the impact is lessened. This fit perfectly to my situation with Emanuele. I needed to let go of my resistance to what was happening. I needed to learn to flow with the changing circumstances of life.

That insight has carried me through many storms in the coming years, and even though it wasn't always easy to do that, to flow, it made a difference each time I did. Thank you again, Mother Nature, for that amazing teaching!

I did a lot of journal writing and I cried a lot at night as I was doing my best to let go. In retrospect what I understand is that this loss of Emanuele catalyzed a cracking of my subconscious where I had so much sadness and hurt that had never had the space to be felt or heard and it was just gushing out because of this experience. I seemed to have an endless ocean of tears in me. I just let them flow as they needed to, without resistance or creating too much story in my mind about it.

I stayed in Haadrin for about five days and decided it was time to go back to Bangkok soon. I had no idea what I would do but I knew something would show up.

It was a sudden decision when I woke up the next morning that I should go right away and catch the water taxi to Tongsala to catch the next ferry at noon. I got my things together as quickly as possible, paid for my stay, and off I went, following that sense of urgency again.

When I arrived at Tongsala and was getting my ticket I saw Emanuele sitting in the restaurant where we had met his friend on our first day. He waved me to come over. He said he was feeling too sad to stay, that he had left me a letter with Oi telling me that and apologizing again.

So he was planning to be on the same ferry as me. What are the odds? So we went together to Bangkok. I was afraid to ask, so I waited to see if we would get a room together or not. He got a room for us. He was loving again and seeking closeness. I opened my heart to him.

He was going to book his flight to the Philippines the next day and asked me what I was going to do. I said I didn't know yet.

The next morning I woke up and heard the words in my head, "Go to Nepal!" I didn't really know anything much about Nepal except the name of the city Kathmandu from when I painted Buddhas eyes on the sign we made. Somehow it felt right to go there, so when Emanuele booked his flight to the Philippines, I booked a flight to Kathmandu.

His flight was leaving in two days, mine was leaving the following week, on December 31, 1991.

As I write this now, I just realized that My trip to Nepal was one year, almost to the day, that I had gone to the World Healing Meditation. Wow! A lot of life had been lived in that year! What an adventure, one I never could have imagined in my wildest dreams. That's the power of opening to the unknown and showing up. Incredible.

I decided I would go back to Seaview Rainbow after Emanuele left to spend Christmas with Loreene and my friends there. Emanuele and I shared the last two days in Bangkok together before he left. We hung out with Chad in the evenings and visited some tourist sites during the day. Things weren't as they once were, but at least we were talking and sharing again. I had a glimmer of hope, but at the same time, focused my energy on letting go and moving on as best I could.

I was so happy to get back to Seaview. They all greeted me with so much love and joy. I realized they all became my family over there. They genuinely cared for me and engaged me with depth and goodness. I continued my Yoga and everything with Loreene and had a beautiful Christmas with everyone. On the 28th I headed back to Bangkok. It was a long trek from the island back to Bangkok, but it was worth it. I travelled by bus this time. What a long ride. I promised myself I would go with the train again next time. It took so much longer to get there and I got motion sickness even though I sat at the front of the bus. Also, during the bus ride, at one point it sounded like there were people moving around under the bus where the luggage was. It seemed implausible to me, but later when I returned to the Guest House I saw that my backpack had been opened and my belongings sorted through. Fortunately I didn't have anything of value in it. I later found out from other travelers that it's a common way of theft in Thailand.

The next day when I was having lunch at what had become my favorite restaurant on Koh Sahn Road, I met a guy named Fred. He was a photographer who had lived in Asia already almost 10 years, just traveling and working. Wow! I thought that was incredible. We had some deep conversations about life and one moment when I was feeling emotional I commented that I wished I could just love myself. He looked at me with a quizzical look and said, "But don't you see? You do love yourself! If you didn't love yourself you wouldn't do all the things you are doing to heal and understand yourself!" I looked at him with a blank look on my face and my tears stopped instantly.

I was speechless. He was right. What a revelation that was. It freed me of the weight of the story I had told myself that I didn't love myself. Incredible! That comment from Fred had such a huge impact that it shook me and got me out of feeling like a victim of my own self perceptions. Sometimes all it takes is one word, one sentence, to shift our inner world into a new direction. Powerful and humbling.

There are some other gems he left me with to that got me thinking and seeing myself in a more loving and kind way. After lunch I focused on getting ready for my flight that night. Sometimes when I reflect on that leap into the absolute unknown I am amazed at the young woman I was. I had no other plans but to arrive at the airport, I trusted everything else would unfold.

4

DIVINE GRACE

"It's about restoring innocence.
The innocence that existed before our first pain.
Before the first time we experienced the need to defend
ourselves, or attack in defense.
When the Purity and Love of God/Creation
flowed and lived through us, vitally, truly,
As it does through every flower, tree and blade of grass.
To get behind and heal the shock and numbness
we are all still in to some degree
from that first experience of violence and hurt,
all the other moments that followed and our reactions to them.
Creating layers upon layers of a self-created identity that lives
separate from our original innocence and heart, our true nature.
The journey is to return to our original state of Grace,
to return to Joy and Love and so be governed,
curious, loving, creative, and playful."
- Journal Entry, Berlin 1998, 27 years old

I t was time to fly to Nepal. My grand new adventure. As
I mentioned before, I didn't really know much about
Nepal except that it's close to India. Some of the other
travelers I had met in Bangkok before leaving warned me
about eating street food in Nepal. They told me that most
people get parasites or amoebas, that I should be very careful

where I eat and get my water from. That is all I knew. I didn't realize it then how courageous it was for me to go there alone, knowing nothing. I was just excited for another adventure. I bought a second-hand guide book the day of my flight to have some references to go by in the month I would be there. And off I went!

It wasn't a very long flight, only about two hours. I slept a little bit and when I woke I was so full of anticipation and excitement I had butterflies in my tummy, I could hardly wait to land.

When I got off the plane and through customs I went straight to a taxi stand and requested, "Take me somewhere I can sleep, please." It was around 10:30 pm. I got into the taxi and we drove through groves of people and cows. It was even busier than Bangkok. Cows are sacred in Nepal, so they are free to go anywhere they want. If they are blocking traffic, you just have to wait! I thought that was awesome! The smells of curry and incense was thick and delicious, the colors of the garments the women wore were spectacular. They all looked like Goddesses! It all felt so magical to me!

It was about a 40-minute drive, filled with awe and wonder to get to the hotel the taxi driver brought me to. I remembered that someone I met before I left Thailand told me about a place called the Tamel area, where the travelers hang out. I asked the Guest House manager where that was and it turned out that is where the driver brought me. I was already in Tamel! Cool.

It was absolutely freezing cold, I was so unprepared. That's where a bit of research would have done me good, but then again, this was a part of the adventure of going into the unknown, I told myself.

I checked into my room to find it wasn't heated and there was no hot water! Yikes! It was now just after 11:30 p.m. as I sat on the edge of my bed and asked myself what am I going to do next? It's late and I'm not sure how it is here at night. Do I just stay here until tomorrow morning or do I get up the courage to go out there on the streets and explore? After all, it was New Year's Eve, what better way to bring in the New Year than venturing into the new world I found myself in.

I decided I would go explore, staying relatively close to the Guest House, but first I lit incense and did a prayer of thanks for this last year of so much growth, healing and adventure and a prayer for the year to come. My heart was so full of gratitude.

I put on as many layers as I could and went outside. Immediately upon walking out the door, I was approached by an aged man begging. I had also been warned about giving money to people begging there, particularly children. I was told there is a kind of mafia-like organization where kids are sent out to beg; that they are taken out of school by their parents, and only a small percentage of the money went to them. I was also told that it is common that some would even intentionally maim themselves in order to beg. This was a devastating reality to see, my heart was so broken seeing so many suffer. I wanted to help in some way, however small.

When this old man came to me, with only a T-shirt on in below-freezing temperatures, I smiled at him warmly and said come with me, we will go into that store and I will buy you a sweater. The store was just getting ready to close but thankfully they let me in. I bought him a really warm sweater and I bought myself a jacket. When I gave it to him, he was very grateful and gave me a beautiful toothless smile. I was also grateful that I could do that. I decided in that moment that I wouldn't give money to those who approached me, but I would buy them food or clothing during my stay there. Which I did. Things weren't too expensive, which made it possible for me to do that.

I continued walking through the village and came upon a jewelry store. What a surprise that was. There was a ring Emanuele had shown me many months before that he had wanted to have one day. It was the Hindu High Priest Ring with semi-precious and precious gems representing the planets, according to Vedic Astrology.

Without him knowing it, I had taken the photocopied picture of it that he had and brought it with me. I wanted to see if I could have one made for each of us there. Bashka had told me Nepal is an inexpensive place to have custom jewelry made when I showed her the picture in my last visit to Seaview Rainbow.

I stood outside this store and contemplated going in to ask if they could make the rings when a young man stepped out and greeted me. We shared pleasantries and I took out the picture from my bag to show him and ask him if they could make that ring. The only thing, I told him, was that there were two stone names in Italian that I didn't know how to translate. All of a sudden he starts speaking Italian to me. What?! He said he knows what stones they are and that they could make the ring. I asked him how he could speak such good Italian. He said there are many Italian travelers so most Nepalese people in Kathmandu, can speak Italian. Well, how about that! Amazing! My first night out and I already found the place to make the rings. Wow!

He invited me into the shop where I met his five brothers. They welcomed me to sit down and then sent for some chai from one of the street vendors. I knew I had been warned not to do that but I decided to take my chances. I wanted to experience the culture with the people. I fell in love my first sip. It was delicious chai. Mmmm.

They were all curious about where I came from, what my work was back home etc., and how I knew about the Ring. We sat together and talked for about 15 minutes, then they wanted to close the store. One of the brothers, Raj, warned me about being on the streets alone at night and offered to chaperone me home. I thought that was very considerate and accepted his offer.

As he locked the door it was almost midnight. He invited me to have a Coke next door where there was a partially covered storefront outside cafe with a fire pit in the middle. I said sure, thank you. We sat down with an older local woman and watched the fire.

So I brought in the New Year in Nepal sitting with a beautiful old woman and my new friend Raj, drinking a Coke around a fire pit. How cool was that!!! I felt so happy to be there. I soaked in every moment and welcomed the New Year with so much joy, hope and gratitude.

When we were done, Raj walked me home and suggested a different guest house that would be closer to the center and less expensive. He said the taxi drivers always take people to the most expensive places because they get a commission. He offered to meet me the next morning and take me there. Again, I said, great. How lucky was I to right away meet these fine people. I felt safe.

Smiling brightly, I entered the Guest House and told the manager I would be leaving in the morning. When I got to my room I washed my face with the ice-cold water, brushed my teeth and dove under the covers as fast as I could. I even had to sleep with my toque! I fell asleep right away and slept deeply the entire night through.

The next morning I had a quick cold shower, then checked out and met Raj at the restaurant that he had pointed out to me the night before. He said they had really good food. *Narayans* was the name. I ate breakfast, then he brought me to the new guest house. I liked it a lot, there were colorful painted murals on the walls, and it was more central, as he had said. There was even a rooftop I could hang out on and write in my journal and watch the stars at night, which I did every night. It was perfect!

Though I was still holding sadness about Emanuele, I was moving forward none the less. I decided to have the rings made in spite of us not being together, as a token of friendship at the very least. He had been an important part of my life that I wanted to honor. I knew he would be really happy to have one. After settling in to my new room I went to the jewelry store and picked out the gems for each ring and gave them my gold earring's so they could melt them for the design of the sun around the ruby in the center. To pick out the stones I used my pendulum. They had never seen anything like that and were greatly intrigued. I explained how the pendulum worked and Raj immediately made himself one with a string and a coin that had a hole in it. It was a fun afternoon.

Afterward, I wanted to go to this famous bookstore where travelers leave their books and get new ones, good quality ones, apparently. A fellow traveler I met in Thailand had told me about it. It truly is an amazing store, I couldn't believe how many books they had. I had thought it would be a tiny store somehow but it was huge! I was looking for some books on Vedic Astrology so that I could learn the meanings and significance of the planets and the gems that were in the ring. The owner helped me find some really good books. I also bought a meditation tape.

In the week that followed I spent a few hours each day in *Narayans,* eating my favorite local dishes while studying at my favorite table by the window. I met a lot of really nice people, had great conversations about life and spirituality. It was amazing to meet so many people on a similar quest of self- awareness. Some also recommended places I could go see nearby.

One day I went to the Monkey Temple. You have to climb about 1000 steps to get to it. It was a beautiful climb with hundreds of other people. The view of Kathmandu was spectacular from up top. The Temple was so old and so beautiful, with the eyes of the Buddha up top, just like the ones I had painted on the sign, which by the way we did complete and erected on the beach with a wind piece made of coconuts at the top. It turned out so beautiful. Now here I was at the temple. Magic.

There were so many monkeys there! I understood why they called it The Monkey Temple. They just come right up to you and you have to be careful that nothing is open in your bag or they steal your things. Quite funny. I felt a deep silence and beauty when I entered the temple, similar to what I feel when I enter the old churches in Europe. Ancient. The amount of prayers those old buildings hold down through the ages. It definitely leaves an energy signature that you can feel when you enter them.

Since I arrived I was experiencing some discomfort in my gut, I was bloating a lot, so I sought out a naturopathic healer, which was something totally new for me. The Sadhu guy I met at Seaview told me about this doctor's clinic in Kathmandu in case I needed a doctor for any reason during my stay.

He had given me the address, so one morning I set out to find him. It wasn't that easy, I had to go down many back and side roads and alleys, I had to ask for directions many times, until I finally found him. As I was waiting in the waiting area, this tall, blonde, beautiful mature woman came in who reminded me of the same wisdom and grace I saw in Iona from the Crystal store in Toronto. I had brought and was reading Lynn Andrews' book where she spoke about a worldwide sisterhood called the "Sisters of The Shields." I knew she had mentioned they were in Nepal, too. I had a sweet innocent wish that I might meet someone and they would invite me to be a part of their collective. When I looked at this woman I wondered if she might be one of the sisters. It's so cute when I think back on it. So eager and earnest I was, still am really.

I was finally called to see the doctor. He said it was good that I came and gave me some interesting looking pellets and a powder I was supposed to take before meals.

After I left I made my way through the maze that brought me there, back to my guesthouse. I was getting very comfortable being in this new place and new culture; even though I was alone, I strangely felt safe. I actually felt at home. I wish I could remember all the names of all the people I met. It was such a rich time for me being there.

Another day I decided to get a rickshaw and go to the temple at Boudhanath. It was about 11 kilometers outside the city center. That was an amazing day. We had to stop and wait for a cow to move at one point. It was sweet experiencing that. I spent the whole day at the temple walking around, watching all the people coming through, the Tibetans doing their mantras, children playing in the streets. It was awe-inspiring. So much life, so much movement. So many human universes interacting, meeting, exploring. I remember I had a few conversations with strangers, all spiritually inclined; I was in heaven! I went to a rooftop cafe when I finished walking all the levels of the temple, sat and read my book and did some journaling. I felt deeply touched by everything and everyone I encountered. I felt so fulfilled and happy. It blew me away that I felt more at home here than in my own country.

When I had told Iona I was going to Nepal she shared with me a mantra I could use while I was there: *Om Mani Padme Hum.* She said that ancient lands such as Nepal can stir and awaken people into new awareness about themselves and life. She said I would be changed by that experience. I could already feel she was right. Something deep was stirring in me. And here I was, travelling this country all by myself at 21 years old; my birthday had occurred a few weeks before. I felt so grateful for it all.

My visa for Nepal was for a month, I was so happy it was for so long and, I was already wishing it could be longer, but back then the longest travel visa you could get was one month. I stayed on the rooftop café until dusk, then caught another rickshaw back to the Tamel area.

One of the mornings after that I was sitting in Narayans with my books, taking notes when a gentleman from Scotland

I had met once before in the restaurant came in and asked to join me, I said yes, of course.

We chatted and he told me of an experience he had near the jungle in Nepal where he was chased up a tree by a Rhinoceros. I looked at him and thought he was joking, because he had made jokes before, so I started laughing. The visual was just so funny. Then he looked me and said, "I'm serious, that happened to me and it was most terrifying, not funny at all." I apologized and he shared the details of his experience. I had no idea there were Rhinos in Nepal. It's so cold. I thought they were only in the jungles of Africa. He told me that in that region of Nepal it is much warmer than Kathmandu.

He shared with me where he and his friends were off to next, a place called Pokhara, at the base of the Himalayan Mountains. It sounded beautiful, I was still waiting for my rings to be done, but I didn't necessarily have to be there to wait for them, so I asked if I could join them. He said sure, that will be great. They were going to go trekking. I had no idea that was one of the main reasons people went to Nepal. I figured I would just stay and enjoy the town of Pokhara as they went to do their trekking adventure. I let Raj and his brothers know where I was going so they wouldn't worry if they didn't see me. Raj had faithfully walked me home at night many times, and the brothers had become like family. They even gave me jewelry to give to my sister because they said if she is my sister she is their sister now, too. So kind and beautiful.

We caught a bus two days later. It was about a nine-hour trip, I think. It was pretty darn long. I had awakened with a mighty cold that morning, so I stacked my handkerchiefs in my bag on the top and checked out of my Guest House to go meet them at Narayans and then go to the bus depot together.

The bus was soooo old, from like the 60's, I am guessing. We sat in the back, it was so bumpy that we each hit our head several times on the roof. No shock absorbers on that bus at all! Strangely I didn't get much motion sickness at all fortunately; often it's the opposite if I sit on the back of a bus. We had gotten there so late that morning that the back was our only option.

My nose would not stop running the whole way. I had to hang my handkerchiefs in the window to dry them so I could reuse them. I know, so gross. But what to do?

We got there around 6:00 p.m. so we went for dinner in this cozy restaurant. It was a really nice place where I ate a filled naan for the first time. Yummy it was! There wasn't any space for me at the guest house where they were, so I sought out a different one for me. I found another with an accessible rooftop. Yahoo! Pokhara was breathtakingly beautiful; the mountains were bigger than any I had ever seen. I couldn't wait to see them in full daylight in the morning. I was looking forward to communing in nature. Even though I was thoroughly enjoying my time in Kathmandu, I could feel the need to slow down, catch up, and be nourished by nature. All the stimulation I had of new experiences and meeting people was exactly what I needed after all that had happened. But I also knew that I was partially escaping feeling the pain and confusion in me. Nature was the perfect medicine. I could already feel the power and energy of the land and mountains.

I had a really good night's sleep that night. I fell asleep playing the meditation music I had bought at the bookstore in Kathmandu. It really took me deep and knocked me out.

When I awoke I had a somewhat warm shower. Oh, that felt good. I was told I could order breakfast on the rooftop. How amazing is that! So I went up there and had a seat. I brought one of my Carlos Casteneda books, *Journey to Ixtlan*, that I picked up in Kathmandu as well. I ordered breakfast and marveled at the beauty surrounding me. I was in a state of breathless awe!

The view was like nothing I had ever seen before, or even since. There is a magic being surrounded by the Himalayan mountains that is so strong it is palpable. The majesty and wise presence of these mountains have been here witnessing life since the beginning, whenever that was. I remembered the mantra Iona had shared with me. I closed my eyes and sang it for a while in deep reverence and gratitude. I could have easily just sat up there all day marveling and drinking in the beauty.

A few minutes later after I ordered breakfast, a Nepalese woman approached me, selling turquoise and semi-precious gemstone jewelry. She was so elegantly beautiful. Her eyes were so warm and kindness streamed from them. Of course, I had to buy a bunch of jewelry from her! We shared many smiles and happy moments as I enthusiastically picked as many pieces as I could afford.

Just as she left my breakfast came. I ate and read a little bit, pausing multiple times to just take it all in. My first impression of Pokhara was wonderful, full of peace and magic.

When I went into the town where the merchants are, though, it felt less wonderful. They seemed much pushier than in Kathmandu to get you in their stores, and the majority lost their friendliness if you didn't buy anything. At least in Kathmandu they still smiled at you. I felt a bit put off by it and decided I wanted to find my Nature spots to retreat into.

It was still exciting getting to see this new place and the people, it just didn't feel as welcoming and comfortable as Kathmandu did. I took it all in, saw the beauty regardless and had some lunch in one of the restaurants. Thankfully, my cold had dried up with the good night's sleep, but I still felt a bit weak so I went back to my guest house and had a rest and read a bit. I would find my nature spots the next day instead when I would feel stronger. They served dinner at the guest house to so I just stayed in that night and planned to explore more the next day.

That morning at breakfast there was young man sitting at one of the tables when I came up to the rooftop. We introduced ourselves and chatted a few moments and went back to our own thing. His name was Roule, he was from Holland. He was a six-foot-five-inch Viking! I don't think I had ever met anyone that tall before. I was reading my encyclopedia of healing crystals I got from Iona called *Love Is in The Earth*. That caught his attention and started a conversation between us. He was curious about what it was about and how crystals and stones can heal us. I could tell he was a nice guy with an open mind and open heart.

He shared with me that he was going trekking in two days. I kind of wish I would have been a bit more prepared so that I could do that too, but there is always another time if I am called to do that. He told me there was a place just down the street where I could rent a bicycle if I wanted to explore. What a great idea! I thanked him for that. We made a plan to meet for dinner that night, as he was going off with some friends somewhere for the day. I liked him. Everyone I have ever known from Holland has been super kind and super fun to be with. I was looking forward to hanging out later with him.

When I finished breakfast I got my things and went to rent the bicycle. I had no idea where to go so I just jumped on, chose a direction and rode that way. This was so fun. Before this I never knew I could be such an enthusiastic explorer. There was a time I used to be uncomfortable going out alone when I lived in Pickering; I always needed and wanted to be with someone. If I was alone I felt very awkward and didn't like it.

I really started loving this new me! It's amazing how putting ourselves in a new environment activates new faculties and capacities we would never encounter in ourselves otherwise. That's why I think travelling is the best thing to do to open our minds, embrace life, and discover who we are.

All the people, smells, incense burning everywhere, loud music playing, there was so much going on in the villages I rode through. And the colors of everything were so bright and beautiful. I kept riding until I hit a dead end at the foot of a smaller mountain. I got off my bike, locked it up and went walking. When I turned a corner I came upon another absolutely breathtaking view. The mountains were layered with rice terraces. Wow! So perfectly sculptured, layer upon layer of rice terraces. I will never forget the feeling when I saw them. It took my breath away again.

I decided to sit there a while and just enjoy the view and peacefulness. That's what I had been craving. About 30 minutes later I heard a very young voice addressing me from behind. I turned around to see a young boy, maybe 10. He asked me if I wanted to go on a day trek. I said I would love to but I was not prepared. He said not the big mountain, a little one. I followed where he pointed his finger and thought sure. How long will it take, I asked him. He said about seven hours. I calculated and it worked with the timing to meet Roule for dinner. It could work. I had my water bottle and some chocolate so I was set. Off we went!

The embrace of nature fed my heart and soul so deeply. It was a beautiful landscape with the rice terraces behind us as we ascended this little mountain. My body melted and my breathe deepened.

For the most part we walked in silence. This was nice for me so I could be with myself and my reflections. Every now and then he would spot a flower, a tree, or a bird and tell me what they were called. It was just what I needed after the previous day being in the town and feeling harassed by the male merchants. It had triggered a reactive vein in me. Now immersed in Nature again was the perfect rhythm and medicine for me to subdue all that had been activated to restore my nervous system. I had become more sensitive to external energies and people since that pot experience in Bangkok. When I was in Nature I was fine, but with people sometimes it was challenging.

We arrived at the top of the mountain. What a view. More beauty. Just when we were beginning our descent we stopped at this sweet clay house. There was an elderly man, whom I assumed was a grandfather, with a little girl, maybe about 4, and a chicken. The sweet old man offered us each a Coke, so we sat and enjoyed the view and their company until we were done. I so loved this! So simple and so very fulfilling. How blessed was I to be able to experience all this? We then made our way down the mountain. On the way I saw a big bird, like an eagle or a condor. It was so beautiful. I soaked in every view, every tree, every flower, and every sound deep into me. I felt a timelessness that instilled such calm and peace in me.

As we drew closer to the bottom we came upon another clay hut of a woman and her children. She invited us for a chai. Again I felt so grateful for all this beauty, grace, and kindness that I encountered that day, every day really since I arrived in Nepal, except in Pokhara.

We stayed for a while,; I watched her as she cleaned her home, and watched her children playing and making toys with whatever they found.

As we got closer to where my bike was parked, my little companion started sharing all the things he wanted from the western world. A Walkman, video games, stuff like that. I looked at him and said, "You know, you may not understand this now, but, you have so many more riches here that we have lost touch with over there. I understand these things are fascinating to you but so much of what you have here I wish we had there."

We got to my bike and I took out some rupees to offer him for taking me for the day. He hadn't asked, but I figured he was probably hoping and counting on it that I would pay him something. I was happy to do it. It's the one time I gave money in my trip there. I figured he was my tour guide for the day, and tour guides get paid to do what they do.

On my bike I went and rode to meet Roule at the Guest House. I got there a few minutes late, but that was okay. Traveler's time is different than city time. I got changed, then we headed back to Pokhara town for dinner. I noticed I did get treated differently being with him. Interesting. Perhaps being a single woman in that small town was interpreted differently. Roule had suggested canoeing over to the restaurant in the lake that was just below the Himalayan mountains. He said it wouldn't take that long and it would be a beautiful journey. I said sure, let's do it. So we went to where we could rent a canoe for only a couple dollars. We got in and Roule started rowing. Could the day get any better? The water, oh how nice it was to be on and near the water. My heart smiled, my body rejoiced.

It's amazing what opens up in life when we open to it, to the new, the unknown. It can be scary too, of course. Each time I did have to overcome little pangs of fear, and each time I did, I was so grateful I had. There is fear that is fabricated by our imaginations, projections, stories, and interpretations, and then there is the real biological fear that is warning us of real danger. Because the biological reaction to both real danger and imagined fears of danger is exactly the same, we need to know our bodies better and do some research to know the difference, otherwise our fears just take over and we avoid leaving our comfort zone. It takes some deep inner excavations to uncover and understand our fear stories that block us from the present moment and the genuine cues of our biology, so we can discern the difference and engage each moment authentically, based on the moment, rather than the past of future fears. As we learn to discern, we become more empowered in our choices and trust our capacity to decide what comes next. Travelling taught me this. It is an ongoing process of learning, as long as we live. This is what I was beginning to learn and understand more and more each day. What's that saying, that all growth happens outside your comfort zone? It's so true.

We were halfway across the lake when it started to rain. There was an incredibly loud bang in the sky and we saw lightning not far away. Roule taught me how to count to determine how close the lightning was. It was just three seconds away! Ahhh! He quickly rowed to the nearest bank on the side of the lake we could reach. We tied the canoe up and went to the closest restaurant to the boat. It was gushing rain by the time we got to the restaurant and we were soaked! We laughed and had a great time enjoying a nice dinner and great conversation. We stayed for about two hours when the rain finally stopped. Back to the boat we went. We had a beautiful canoe ride back, returned to our starting point and returned the boat to the boys who had rented it to us. What a fun experience!

Unfortunately, Roule was leaving the next morning. I would really miss my new friend, we got along so well. He came by my room to say good-bye and he gave me a stone that he had carried with him from one of his treks and wished for me that it bring me all the luck and peace in the world. That was so sweet and touched my heart. He was such a nice guy; I was so happy to have shared that time with him and for his suggestions that made my stay so beautiful.

The next morning I had breakfast on the roof top again. I couldn't get enough of that majestic view. I decided I was going to rent a bike again and explore the opposite direction. I didn't get far when I came across a river with very high banks. I parked my bike and walked toward it. I encountered an old woman, for sure in her 70's or more, carrying a bushel of long grass bigger than her body. It was incredible. There were other women also carrying heavy loads on their heads. As they passed me they sent me warm smiles. I found the Nepalese women so regal and beautiful. I also encountered the sweetest little girl when I went to cross over the bridge so I could walk along the river. She was sitting on the ledge exploring her toes with great intensity. It was so beautiful, and I felt privileged to witness the profound moment of discovery she was having with herself. Absolutely precious! She looked at me with her big wide eyes. I gave her a big smile, she just watched me. I wondered why she was there alone when I heard other voices and I saw who I assumed was her mother and other siblings washing their laundry in the river. There was something so beautiful about that entire scene.

As I walked along a path leading me above and along the river, two young men stopped me and asked me if I wanted to go to Davies Falls, a tourist attraction there. I kindly said no thank you, waved my hand good-bye and kept walking.

A short distance in I found a beautiful spot to sit where I wanted to meditate. I was just settling in when on the opposite side of the river I saw these two men again. I got a nervous feeling inside, and hoped they were just on their way somewhere else. Then they stopped almost directly across from me. They yelled across the river "Are you sure you don't want to go to Davies Falls?" I yelled across I was sure. Thank you. Please leave me alone.

They paused, looked at each other, then asked again. Oh my God! What is this? I yelled even louder, this time just a loud NO! They looked at each other again then went off walking. Phew. I closed my eyes to start meditating. About 10 minutes later I opened my eyes and saw one of those men just a little farther away and he was starting to walk down the bank to cross the river and come up close to where I was. I was both angry and nervous now. He came up, I looked at him and yelled, "PLEASE! LET ME BE!" "Okay! Okay!" he said. "I just needed to cross." *Okay, Fine,* I thought.

He thankfully passed by me a few meters away, but then kneeled down, looked at me and asked again, "Are you sure you don't want to go to Davies Falls?" I was shaking in disbelief. I yelled again, "Yes I am sure!" He finally got up and left. Oh, boy, my blood was boiling. What was with that? Such a strange encounter. I decided I was going to go back to my bike and perhaps just go to my guest house for a rest to recover from that experience. It really stressed me out.

As I was walking back I noticed the family that had been doing their laundry was no longer there. It was a beautiful big rock they had been on, and I love big beautiful rocks! It was right at the entrance to where my bike was, so I decided I would be okay and went down to the rock. *My thick wool socks needed a washing for sure*, I thought I laid out my poncho, the sun was pleasantly beaming hot. I sat down, took my boots off and washed my socks. What a simple pleasure that was for me.

I took a few deep breaths and decided to lie back while my socks dried in the sun. A few minutes later I heard a sound to my right. I opened my eyes to check and it was just a goat climbing the river bed. Such a cutie, he looked at me, I looked at him and then I went, "Bahahaha!" I love making animal sounds, trying to connect with them. I laughed at myself, and the goat just looked at me. Funny moment. Silly human! I closed my eyes again and was able to rest for about 20 minutes when I heard sounds to the left of me which is where the path was to come down to where I was. It was one of those young men, the other one.

As soon as I saw him I start getting my things together, put my boots on without my socks and got up and headed toward another little path that would lead me up. He was coming down and asked me if I had a partner. Sarcastically I said, "Yes, he is at Davies Falls!!!" Oh so funny! He proceeded to ask me if I wanted to have relations with him. Whoa!!! What!?! Now that was really weird! I said "No!" and kept walking up my little path. He followed me, somehow totally bewildered that I said no and said, in all seriousness, "But Ma'am, I can finger, I can screw, I can lick, I can suck and I can fuck."

Oh my God! I burst into laughter and said, Well, good for you but I don't want any." By that time, I had reached the top of the path. His other friend had appeared. I yelled at the top of my lungs that they may be able to treat their women like trash but not me, and it's not right how they treat their women!

Suddenly they turned all meek: "Okay Ma'am, good-bye Ma'am," and walked away. I was absolutely dumbfounded and perturbed by that encounter, but so grateful nothing worse came of it.

Later when I shared my experience with another traveler, the person told me that it wasn't uncommon for single white women to seek out the company of young Nepalese boys. I realized my first mistake when I encountered them while I was entering the path along the riverbed. I was friendly when I said no thanks, and I had waved good-bye to them. That day I learned that over there a "soft no" is like a "hidden yes." Unless you are strong and clear in your "no," they just keep at you until you assert yourself clearly. But what a proposition he had rehearsed. Bless. Again, I am grateful that in the end, they were harmless.

My nerves were frazzled after that. I remembered the canoe ride the night before, how peaceful that was. I thought that's what I needed, some peaceful time on the water. I got on my bike and went to where Roule had rented the canoe so I could rent it again, hoping it would be available.

They had been respectful last night when I was with Roule; tonight, however, they were being jerks taunting and teasing me with chauvinistic comments. I just wanted to get in the canoe. I gave them the money and got in.

Yesterday they gave us a push because the canoe was partly in the mud so we could board it. Today they didn't give me a push and were laughing at me thinking I wouldn't make it out on my own. I tell you, I dug the oar into the mud with all my might and pushed as hard as I could until I was free and I rowed off. They didn't expect that. They were suddenly quiet.

Ahh, finally some peace and quiet. I rowed to the middle of the lake and just sat there soaking in the silence, coming gradually back down from both those experiences.

I didn't want to stay in Pokhara another day. That, I decided, was a certainty. I stayed out on the water until dusk. When I brought the boat back there was only one guy there. He was quiet as a mouse. I went for a bite to eat and then straight back to the Guest House. What a day. I wanted out of there. I grabbed my guide book for Nepal for the first time since I arrived that I had bought in Thailand,. I went and sat on the toilet to read it, closed my eyes and opened it up to a page. I looked at the pictures and thought that would be nice, down south by the jungle. A place called Chitwan Park.

I went to the manager of the Guest House a bit later and said I wanted to leave the next day. I asked him if he could arrange my ticket on a tourist economy bus. He said yes, he told me how much it would cost, and I gave him the money. Great!

He came back to my room and told me my bus left very early in the morning at around 5, and he would take me to the bus depot at 4. It felt so good knowing I would be leaving the next day.

Next morning he knocked on my door, ready to go. I was pretty tired still but got my stuff together and off we went. Oh my goodness! We got to the so-called bus depot. It was a big parking lot with no signs, no bus numbers and no other travelers, just locals. It was still pretty dark out and hard to make anything out. There were also lots of chickens. He told me to wait a minute and took my bag with him. Uhh? What just happened? I was in the middle of nowhere, he had my bag and there was no one I could speak to for help who understands me. I prayed I could trust him and that I and everything would be okay. I waited for what felt like an eternity.

Thankfully, a few minutes later he did return. He pointed to the bus I needed to go on. I could see my backpack on the top of it. This was definitely not a tourist economy bus, this was a local bus, which is fine by me except I had paid him for the other bus, which was much more than what the fee would be for this one. I started asking him about this and he said it's all okay, that he had to go, avoiding answering me completely. So he ripped me off! Another unpleasant Pokhara experience to finish my time there off. I was so happy to get away from there.

I went to the bus, got on right away and sat in the second row. In the first row was a lady with her chicken. To my side was a lady with her goat. It was a fun new experience. The bus filled up, and I was the only Western person on it. No one spoke English, either.

Okay. It would be a six-hour bus ride, *I'll be ok* I thought to myself. What an adventure. We finally took off. The bus stopped in many places and picked up more people who climbed up top as well. I thought of my backpack. I did an inventory in my head of all the important things I had in my body wallet, making sure I had everything that was important. I took a deep breath, letting go of the fears that were attempting to take over. I thought. maybe it will be there when we get there, maybe it won't. I have the essentials and I will be okay. I had to let it go, otherwise the bus trip would have been just me being afraid. How could I enjoy anything like that? Once I did release the fears I started enjoying the sights and landscapes we were passing through. They were astounding!

Nepal was truly beautiful. For the most part, the locals were gentle and kind people. I still felt a little uneasy with no other travelers around and nobody speaking English, but I was adapting.

The bus made a stop a few hours later in a bustling little town. The streets were full of people. Still not a traveler in sight, all just locals. Everyone got off the bus to get a drink or use the hole in the floor to go to the bathroom. I felt nervous about getting out, I had no idea when the bus planned to leave, afraid it could leave without me, also being a lone woman and a foreigner ... oh boy ... but I had to go pee though! I had to overcome my fear and just get off the bus and go into the closest restaurant. So I did.

I used their hole in the floor, bought myself a Coke and went right back onto the bus. I watched the people outside as I drank my Coke and thought about Emanuele. Wondering how he was, what was he doing in the Philippines. A bit of sadness came over me for a moment but I shook it off, and kept enjoying the view and the people.

I was kind of happy to be on that bus now rather than the tourist one, even if I was a bit scared. I was able to be with the people of Nepal. Many smiled, kindness flowing from their eyes, and curiosity, too. Back then there weren't as many travelers as there are now. There were no cell phones and there was no internet. I am really happy I got to experience Nepal before it grew into a tourist destination, and before the technology made it impossible to truly get away. Same with Thailand. Koh Pahn Gang has changed too and now has a freeway running through it. I shudder at the thought of it. My beautiful Gilligan's Island, totally developed now. I can't even imagine. I've heard Nepal has changed a lot too, over the years. What a blessing to have traveled before all the development happened.

I was in my reverie, watching the life before me, when a little girl came and tapped me on the shoulder. At first I didn't realize what she wanted, then she looked at the Coke bottle. The bus was filling back up so I guessed we were leaving soon. I drank down my last few sips and with a smile gave her the bottle. She gave me a sweet smile back. Simple moments of grace and beauty. Those are my favorite.

We drove a few hours and were now climbing a mountain road that seemed way too narrow for this bus. Then, all of a sudden the bus broke down; fortunately, though, there was a wider side road area the driver rolled the bus into.

We had to wait until he fixed it. Everyone got out of the bus and just stood outside waiting. Down below was a river, it sounded beautiful. A nice place to get stuck, for sure! As I was admiring the trees and nature around me I was jolted into a very different reality. As my view moved back toward the bus and I saw some of the people started just going to the bathroom where ever they were. Not just Number One, either! Oh my! I had never experienced that before. Interesting. No one seemed to mind. It was just the way they did it. Okay, then.

A little bit later a young boy from a neighboring village came around, selling papadams, chick-pea crunchy bread. I bought a few, they were so yummy. There goes the rule of not eating street food again! By the looks of it he was on his way walking to the next town where he was going to sell them. So far I had been okay even with having eaten coconut and other street snacks in my bus travels. Finally someone came to help the driver, they fixed the bus and we were on our way. Yay! It took about two more hours to get to the town where I had to transfer, Tadi Bazaar was the name of the village.

When we got there I was informed that the only way to get where I wanted to go was by ox car. *Wow! Really? Amazing! How cool is that!* I thought to myself. It would be a three-hour ox-car ride and I was the only passenger. I couldn't help but think of Emanuele at different times. We had been best friends, so of course I wanted to be able share my adventures, like this one. That thought brought a bit of sadness up in me again, it was an almost constant wrestling match within me to not get caught and drown in it, but I shifted my attention to the beauty of the moment the best I could.

I marveled at this little way point in my journey, the people selling food, clothing and drinks to those of us passing through. I went to get some more water and use the hole in the ground and off we went. Such extraordinary beauty! Spectacular!

It was the time of year when the mustard fields were blossoming. Oh my, the colors! The bright yellow and contrasting green was breathtaking, and there were miles and miles of these fields. It was like a celebration and here I was in the middle of it. The oxen were so big and beautiful too, they have the sweetest eyes with big eyelashes.

The driver didn't speak much English so it was silence most of the time. Perfect. I loved it and soaked every bit of the beauty in that I could. I am so grateful that I never lost my connection to Nature. Even the slightest moments nourished me so deeply and kept my hope and faith in the good in life alive. Whenever I felt like giving up, which happened often for a period of time, witnessing the beauty and resilience in Nature came to my rescue every time. In watching Nature, I realized that we all experience the same changes and cycles. That we *are* Nature. We have sunny days, rainy days, inner tsunamis, electrically charged days and the cycles of life, death, fermentation, and rebirth, when we go through experiences that change us. Also, we experience a life-giving force that supports our growth and wants us to fulfill the true expression of our unique soul and being. This universal force is all-giving, all-loving, and all-supportive. The name we give it is arbitrary. The same life giving force as in Nature. This force existed before humanity, before we could even attempt to create words and stories to interpret and name it. And it will exist long after we are gone. It's pure love and wisdom. Nature.

In Hawaii, there is a wisdom shared that says Heaven is not a place, that it's a frequency. They understand that the Kingdom of Heaven is here on Earth already, that the entire natural kingdom is still vibrating in the frequency of Heaven, and is just waiting for us to wake up to our true essence and return to that frequency. For me, that makes a lot more sense than any other story I have heard. It resonated deep within me when I encountered that teaching. That's clearly why we all feel so good when we are in Nature. Even science has proven that just 20 minutes in Nature reduces stress in people.

Sitting in that wooden ox car, I felt heaven on earth all around and within me. Those three hours went by way too fast for me.

We arrived to the edge of the jungle close to dusk. The driver took me to a guest house. It seemed all right. I ate dinner there, but the young guys were weird with me. I decided I had had enough of that in Pokhara, so I was going to look for another place the next day. At breakfast, another traveler told me about a place right at the edge of the jungle by the river. That sounded really appealing. After breakfast I headed that way by foot, hoping I had the directions right. After about 20 minutes I found it. It was so nice! They had individual clay huts for rent that were roundish in shape like a cave and looked really cozy. Felt like a womb of the Earth. Perfect! I asked if they had any vacancies, they had only a double room for two nights that is shared with someone else, but then I could have my own hut after that. Awesome!

I shared the big space with an American guy, I think his name was Dave. There was no electricity, and the shower was outside with a little hut for meals. Nice. I liked that a lot, more time in Nature. At night time it was lit up with kerosene lanterns and candles. Lovely.

I was really exhausted once I had my place to settle. Those unpleasant experiences in Pokhara had kind of picked at my vulnerability and I felt sadness around all the changes with Emanuele.

The first two days, I cried so much. Everything I was pushing aside so I could be present to enjoy the moment, all came gushing out once I was settled in. It was like waves of a lifetime of repressed and suppressed emotion came flowing out of me with the sadness about Emanuele.

It's how it works. When we are in a momentum of change and movement for a period of time, then once we slow down or stop, what we have been suppressing catches up with us and we at long last have to encounter, feel, and heal the emotional pains emerging. No matter how I tried I couldn't stop the pain and tears. With that anger at life and God came up creating a tone of bitterness that I had never experienced before.

I think I came across as really unfriendly the first two days with the other people there, I was so withdrawn in myself.

Dave approached me the second day and asked me why I was crying so much. I shared what was happening, the shock of loss, the pot that messed with my head, my mom and everything that was troubling me.

He was very kind, and shared some comforting words of support and advice. He got me to smile a bit again. He said things I essentially already knew, but, when I was caught in my inner tsunami, how easily I forgot to use my knowledge to turn the light back on inside me. I was so grateful; his kindness and care made a difference.

I was writing in my journal every day. Reflecting on my life, questioning reality, who I thought I was, who I was becoming, all kinds of deep inquiries. I was changing, a lot. I was no longer the girl I once was.

My whole inner world was shifting and was still somewhat unfamiliar to me. All the outer changes were rippling into my inner landscapes and I was shaken up with no clear identity or foundation anymore to help me stay anchored in the flux. My heart was still my heart, still kind, still loving and caring, but my mind was all over the place.

While writing in one of my journals, it occurred to me that many of my thoughts and beliefs and views of the world I had actually inherited from my family. They weren't authored by me. I was looking into what was really authentically me. My thoughts, my experience, my beliefs etc. -- even my beliefs about myself -- were seen through their perception of me that I took to be true and made them a part of my self-definition.

I also felt a lot of anger come up in me around those real-izations. This was way deeper than just the separation with Emanuele. That experience was merely a catalyst revealing what was buried in me all along.

I realized that the separation hit me so hard because I had let him into the deepest place in my heart, the part of my heart that had shut down all those years ago that had reemerged with his love and our friendship. In a way it felt like I was becoming re-traumatized. The abandonment wound in me opened to the surface but I didn't know how to define it at that time, nor how to heal it. I would have emotional releases, but they only temporarily relieved the building pressure in me; the core remained raw and unhealed. It was a long day of emoting and processing. Journaling and being in Nature helped immensely, as always. Where would I be without the love and inspiration of Nature?

The next day Dave left and I was given my own hut. I was starting to feel a bit lighter, changing my focus again to where I was and the beauty around me. Most of the days I just sat outside at a wooden table made from an ox car wheel that still had the handles attached making it look like a wheel barrow that's the best way I can describe it. It was located not far from the river, so beautiful and the perfect place for writing in my journal and reflecting on life. Everyday these sweet kids, two girls and a boy, would just hang out with me. They would play around me and laugh at the silliest things. I dropped my bottle of water once and they burst into uncontrollable laughter! They were so lovely and brightened my heart every day. They brought me healing by inspiring me to connect to my own innocence and the simple joys of interacting and being Human.

Across the river was the jungle. Elephants, rhinos, tigers, and so many more incredible creatures literally just meters away. Apparently at night they often came across the river to where we are. We were warned to not go outside at night for that reason.

My first night in my hut in the middle of the night I suddenly heard laughter outside. It sounded like people. I wondered what are they doing being outside at night and laughing so loud? It sounded like at moments they were right behind my hut.

The next day I asked, Mahdu, the helper who or what that was that I heard, he said they were hyenas. Holy cow! Apparently there had also been a rhino coming over at night recently. Amazing. But I sure didn't want to go outside when they were there!

There were a few shops made of basic plywood close by in the village that I walked to most days. In one of them I would drink my tea or coffee, another I could buy chocolate and snacks, and one other one had books for sale. There was only one little restaurant type of place that also had tea as well and snacks.

On one of my wanderings In a nearby village I came upon a celebration of some kind where they were dancing around a big bon fire. One of the people saw me and invited me to join. I danced my heart out around the fire. What a release and joy it was. I envisioned Native Peoples in the past dancing in ceremony around the fire. How they connected to Nature and Spirit and expressed emotions through sound and movement. They danced to celebrate, to mourn, to pray, to welcome a union or a new child to the community. How freeing and beautiful I thought to have such a means of processing the myriad of experiences we go through in a lifetime. It made me reflect how little opportunity we have in my 'culture' to do that. Everything just gets pushed down. No wonder there is so much dis-ease in our Western World.

I felt emptied and full after the dancing when I headed back to my hut at dusk. Seeing these happy people celebrating so profoundly fed and nourished my heart as well. I was reconnecting to my love of humanity and life, full of Gratitude.

One day two women arrived, Simone and Simone, both from Holland. It was cute that they had the same name. We hit it off right away and spent our remaining time there together.

One day I brought them to the shack restaurant to have tea. There was an old man there smoking a water pipe. He showed us a game called Bhaga Chal, it's like a Nepalese version of chess. It's their national game.

You have four sheep and 21 tigers. The sheep have to trap the tigers so they can't jump and eat the sheep; and the the tigers objective is to eat the sheep. Apparently the odds are equal. Simone played with him first, then we all played many games. It was a lot of fun.

They were very conscious women, so we had some deep and profound conversations that were healing and nourishing for me. We laughed a lot too, which made the connection even more beautiful and very balanced. My joyful heart was coming back on line.

We decided to get a guide to take us on a jungle walk one day. It was the season where people came from all over Nepal to burn and cut the long grass that they used for fixing their homes, making baskets, whatever they needed it for. We came upon many little groups and families on our walk and often stopped to drink a chai with them. They had made little earth ovens to cook and heat the tea. It was amazing. Again I observed the Nepalese women as being very regal and elegant in their movements and mannerisms. They looked gentle, but you could see they were very strong, as well.

At one point close to the end of the day and our walk we came around a corner of long grass and there stood a rhinoceros, maybe 20 feet away. We froze on the spot. Our guide instructed us to very slowly move toward the tree on our right, to not move fast, or the rhino could charge. I thought of the Scottish man I had laughed at when he told me he had been chased up a tree. Oh boy. *Instant karma,* I thought! We got to the tree as fast as possible, going slowly of course, and could see the rhino sniffing the air as we got to it. Rhinos are blind to anything beyond 10 feet, so they are known to just charge at anything unfamiliar. He was catching our scent and coming in our direction. Simone and Simone got up the tree with great speed. But me with the rhino coming closer, I froze in fear, I couldn't move. The guide had to shove his walking stick up my butt to get me up. It was as terrifying as the Scotsman described. We all got up in the tree and had to simply wait until he no longer caught our scent now that we were higher, and wait for him to go.

It took a while until he finally turned around and started heading the other direction. We stayed in the tree waiting for him to be far enough away before we got down. Our guide obviously knew there was a camp of people behind the grass in the direction the rhino was going, so he let out a big yell, screaming a few words to the people behind the grass that we couldn't see. Just seconds later, two trees where the people were got filled with people. It was almost comical how fast they all got up there as soon as he hollered. Apparently at least 100 deaths happen a year by a rhino charging blindly at what he can't recognize. Once we got down from the tree, we walked a bit more then went back to the hut. The next day we rode elephants into the jungle to get a safer view from above. I love elephants. I was told the elephants we were riding were owned by a local family who treated them well. I can only hope that was true, otherwise I wouldn't have gone.

We came upon two large rhinos. One of them had a big gash in its hind right leg, like he had been fighting with another rhino, perhaps. They are incredible creatures. I found them quite beautiful the more I looked at them. We came across a few other animals that I no longer know the names of. It was a great experience and a great day again. Both Simones were very kind and supportive when I would have moments of processing. They were a saving grace for me that I could share what I needed to in order to learn and grow from my experiences.

Another day we walked into a neighboring village. There were a lot of children. A traveler I had met in Thailand before going to Nepal told me that the girls love hair elastics and all the kids love pens and candies, so I had stocked up in Kathmandu before I left. As we were walking through the town the children circled us while walking with us. One girl pointed to my hair elastic so I gave it to her. Then I reached in my pockets and threw everything I had in the air so it would be like a game for them. They laughed. Such beautiful innocence and purity I felt from these children.

We then walked to an elephant farm. I was so sad to see what I saw there. There was a baby elephant tied up, and the mother was tied up as well, far enough away that the baby couldn't reach her. That broke my heart. The baby and the mother kept swinging their bodies back and forth trying to reach each other. Terrible. I cried. I was sitting on a bench and an old elephant was being walked right passed me. It was like the elephant was reading my thoughts of wonderment that such large and noble creatures could be ruled by us scrawny humans. I looked into its one big blue eye, which is apparently very rare, and it felt like he was saying, we are tolerating this for now humans, but one day we won't.

I got chills and sent love to the elephants and prayed for them and for Humanity to wake up to see the harm they are causing to animals and Nature. We left shortly after my encounter with the elephant.

Then nine days had gone by since I arrived and it felt like time to go back to Kathmandu. Simone and Simone were going to go to India; they invited me to join them but it didn't feel right for me at that time. Also, I only had another week left in my visa for Nepal, and wanted to be in Kathmandu. We took the ox car together to Tadi Bazaar. That was fun, and then we went our own ways.

I observed a big change in me. I used to be really emotional with good-byes, but I didn't feel anything. I wasn't sure however if it was because my heart was protecting itself or if I was just no longer that emotionally attached and it was good. It may have been a bit of both.

I got on the bus pretty much right away when we arrived. Mahdu, the helper, also caught the bus to Kathmandu. We had all become friends. He was sweet, but I could tell he had a crush on me so I had to be careful to not be too friendly.

It was nice to be back in my familiar neighborhood of Kathmandu. I saw many people I now knew as friends and some of the shop owners too. It was so much easier there. Once again, I spent a lot of time at Narayans restaurant reading and studying Vedic Astrology in my remaining days there.

I met a guy from Italy named Nino. We hung out quite a bit. He took me somewhere I could buy some really nice turquoise. I went with my pendulum and purchased several pieces to bring back with me and give as gifts.

One night he was supposed to meet me at Narayans. He was very late and it was coming close to closing time and was already dark outside. Raj had already gone home since I told him Nino would walk me to the guest house.

A few times over the past hour I saw a man moving from one place to the other outside, but from each position I noticed he was watching me. I was starting to get really nervous. Fifteen minutes before closing this man walked into the restaurant and sat at the table beside me. I got uncomfortable shivers up my spine. He was Nepalese and rough looking. I pretended I didn't notice him. "*Where are you Nino?*" I yelled at him in my mind.

Five minutes before closing, he finally showed up. Phew. I was already shaking by the time he came in. As soon as he sat down, the man at the table beside me stood up and walked out. I looked at Nino about to share about the man ; he said "You don't have to tell me. The look on that man's face when he saw me sit with you told me everything. He was clearly disappointed and had something not good in mind for you." Oh man, close call. God knows what that man had planned for me when I stepped out alone. That was the only moment in the whole month that I felt in danger. Except for the Rhino.

At a different restaurant one night a met a woman named Bonnie from the United States. We hit it off splendidly. She was a volunteer teacher at one of the Mother Teresa homes for children recovering from Tuberculosis. I asked her if I could volunteer some of my time in my last days there. She said for sure.

I was only helping for three days but already when I arrived on my second day the children ran to me with so much joy and love, climbing all over me. It was such a beautiful experience. It touched my heart deeply. I wished I could stay longer. We taught them to draw and sing childhood songs that we grew up with. It was pure magic.

The night before I left, when I picked up my rings, which turned out so beautiful, one of the brothers invited me to his home where his wife and brothers put on a feast for me to say good-bye. I was so touched. The one brother even sang some Ragas, spiritual songs from their tradition, for me. The food was delicious but sooooo hot! I had to eat very slowly. As Raj walked me home, I was starting to feel sad to go. What an incredible and full month I had lived.

The next day I went to the airport with a guy I had met when I bought the turquoise. We had run into each other the night before and discovered we had the same flight back, so we decided to travel together. And a good thing we did. When I got to the customs guard, he said I had stayed two days longer than I was supposed to. I thought, *That can't be.* At the travel agency in Bangkok I said I wanted to stay one month. Turns out they made an error.

The border guard pointed that out to me. He wanted to see my bank receipts for changing currency those two extra days.

The law was that for the first month you don't have to show your bank receipts, but after the first month you do, you have to change $100 U.S. a day in order to stay longer. That's how it was then. I had no bank receipts, I had changed all my money on the black market like I was advised to do by Raj because you got triple the amount for your money. I could feel the blood draining from my face. And I had no more money. The guy I came with was behind me; I looked at him, not knowing what to do. He reached into his wallet and handed the guard some money, at which time he stamped my passport and let me go. Whoa! What would have happened if I hadn't gone with him?

There were so many blessings on this journey. So many serendipities. I was so grateful for his kindness, and he didn't even ask that I pay him back either. I offered to send him a cheque and he said no, he was happy to help. Extraordinary.

Even though on the news we keep getting inundated with one terrible act of humanity after another, there is still so much goodness in the world, so many people moved to help others. I remember something I read somewhere that struck a deep chord in me. It went something like this: When there are tragedies in the world, always direct your focus to the helpers, there are always so many helpers who rise to the occasion. We need to give them our full attention, not the disaster nor the sick mind that did something terrible to others. Seeing the helpers will keep us feeding the energy of good, and that is what will prevail.

I like that a lot. It reminds me of a Hawaiian expression, "Love prevails all trauma."

It's something to really take in and think about and direct ourselves to shift our attention in the right direction. Otherwise when we just focus on the negative, the negative is what grows, not love or good. We need to have our eyes open to what is happening in the world, but not to the point that it blinds us from seeing the good. I had experienced so much goodness in Nepal, regardless of the few things that happened in Pokhara. The bigger picture was way more beautiful, crowned by this generosity of a stranger. Simply wow!

5

LIKE ALICE IN WONDERLAND

Nothing happens to me unless I let it,
unless I invite it into my life.
One way or the other,
Good or bad,
It all starts with me.
There are no accidents.
I attract and create my reality.
Both consciously and unconsciously.
- Journal Entry December, 1992, Thailand, 22 years of age.

I t was just before dusk when I arrived in Bangkok. I got a taxi and went back to Koh Sarn Road where I would see if there was a room available for me at Guest House 59. In the lobby area where people check in there is a large chalkboard where they write the names of the people staying and which rooms they were in. As I shot a glance at it I saw the name Emanuele. My heart fell through the floor. Could it be? I thought, No way! He was supposed to be in the Philippines for two more months, according to the plans he shared with me.

Just in case it was him, I wrote a note and put it on his door, letting him know I would be at the restaurant down the street grabbing a bite to eat. I sat in the restaurant waiting, wondering, what if it is him, what will happen? What will it be like? I wrote all my thoughts and feelings in my journal. I had massive butterflies in my stomach. About an hour later, he walked in. I was floored. My entire month in Nepal raced through my mind; it almost felt like a dream. Now here I was and so was he. What are the odds we would arrive on the same day? He had just arrived that morning.

It seemed inconceivable that we kept meeting each other like this. Destiny? Whatever it was that kept pulling us to the same time and same place was pretty magical. He said if I wanted to, I could stay in his room. That surprised me. I thought, *What does that mean? Are we back together?* I was so nervous.

As a way to divert and distract energy and attention, I dug into my bag and got him to close his eyes and put out his hands. I then placed the ring in them. He opened his eyes and was speechless. His fit him perfectly and he loved it. I showed him mine too. Somehow that helped my nervous energy to dissipate. We started sharing about our journeys and it started to feel really good being in each other's company again.

We spent a few days together in Bangkok. I had taken many pictures in Nepal, so I was eager to develop the films. I dropped them off at a photo shop and then we went to the Thai Connsulate to renew our travel visa. We got our stamp in our passports and were all set. We were getting along well, he felt more like the person I knew in Switzerland. After leaving the Consulate we decided to go back to Seaview and booked our tickets. Seaview had become for both of us our home away from home. I was also really looking forward to seeing Loreene again and continue learning with her. I hoped she was still there. When you are a traveler things can change on a whim when nothing is holding you in one place. I knew it was her plan to still be there, but ya never know!

When I picked up my pictures, it felt really surreal and weird. A bit like how I felt when I smoked that pot, dissociated and disconnected.

A whole month I lived there on my own, travelling and getting to know me in a new way. Now, I was back here with Emanuele again and it all felt like a dream. I shared that with him and he said he felt the same thing. Like it was an alternate reality or something. Twilight Zone, mind-bending kind of experience.

I could clearly feel the differences in me in spite of feeling out of it. My confidence had grown immensely compared to when I first arrived in Thailand when I was so fearful. I was still hoping that somehow we would come together again, but was also more grounded in accepting we might not.

We headed back to the island. He seemed more at ease with me again. Somehow I thought maybe because I had gained my independence and was less clingy, he felt more comfortable and had grown some respect for me.

Loreene was thankfully still there in the house across from Seaview. She planned to be there for at least a year she said.

I continued my yoga and meditation classes with her. It was good to be back. Emanuele and I came back together somewhat and just hung out and made jewelry during the day and had a relaxing time for the next month and a half. Oi took us on an overnight fishing trip to a small island not far from where we were. I call it Crab Island because at night there were hundreds of crabs everywhere. They would walk right over you.

Oi went diving for sea urchins. I wasn't much for seafood, but discovered while I was there that when the fish was fresh out of the ocean I actually really enjoyed it. I felt kind of squeamish about eating raw sea urchin, but he made it like a kind of ceviche, cooking it with lime juice. I thought I would at least try it.

Turns out I enjoyed it. The island was so small that I was able to walk around it. In the center were really high ridges. It was beautiful. I spent many hours alone on the opposite side of where Oi and Emanuele were. I just gazed at the stars, connected to nature and prayed for guidance. It was very magical and peaceful. We stayed on the rocky island until dawn and then headed back.

I was still processing so much, so the ease of being by the water with no schedule to be anywhere did me good.

I also spent a lot of time going to a beautiful sweet-water lake I found one day when I went exploring that was just a 10-minute walk away from the bungalow. It was so beautiful and such a perfect place to go to have space to reflect and have my own space.

For many years I had a bit of fear of going into deep water that I wanted to overcome, so I decided to do floating exercises in the shallow water to gain my comfort. I would hold my breath and roll up into a ball and just float. It was like being in the womb. Learning to feel how the water actually held me and supported me was incredibly liberating. It brought me deep healing when I could finally let go and trust I was safe.

Emanuele was being more himself, though still a bit distant. I just did my own thing and learned to go with the flow, which in itself was a huge step for me. We were getting along; that meant a lot for me and gave me hope.

One day, this guy came and rented a bungalow at Seaview. He was alone and had a physical disability where he walked with canes. He was maybe in his mid-twenties, closer to Emanuel's age. I found him to be quite a bitter and angry person and didn't enjoy his presence at all. He and Emanuele became quick friends though. I didn't get a good feeling about him at all. Through that friendship Emanuele started drinking and smoking a lot of pot again because this guy did. Within days the whole painful cycle from the months before started all over again.

I started spending even more time at the lake, reflecting, crying, writing, and playing with my new tarot cards that I had barely touched since we got there. I was desperately trying to understand what was happening and why. The bit of solid ground I thought I had gained was now shaking again, but being at my lake soothed the inner trembling and helped me temporarily feel grounded in myself again.

I also overcame my fear of water at my lake. My floating practice also really helped my nervous system to become more settled. I felt very much at peace when I floated. Eventually I gained the confidence and courage to swim around the circumference of the lake and then eventually right across it. It was an amazing victory and liberation for me. Symbolically, water represents emotions, and the subconscious. As I was overcoming my physical fear of water I was also learning to overcome and heal my internal fears and emotions.

There were always new people coming and going from the Seaview Rainbow. A single woman arrived not too long after that guy and immediately began flirting with Emanuele like crazy. I really had to learn to navigate the paranoia that surfaced in me that he was going to go with her. I sometimes wonder if he might have, he became more and more distant and cold again. It was brutal.

One day he decided to leave Seaview for about five days to do a scuba-diving training up island. In that time he was away I started venturing more and more on my own, even walking all the way to Tongsala, which was more than an hour's walk.

It did me good to be in a different environment and meet other people. I treated myself to a few nice new sarongs and a beautiful bright yellow dress.

Almost every day, I also walked the opposite way up island to one of the other bungalows that had a restaurant and made some friends there.

My inner world was shaking again, surprisingly even more than the first time, I did all I could to remain calm and practice letting go. At one moment I realized, like the metaphor with the waves, letting go was the only option I had if I didn't want my emotions to escalate and shake me even more. If I fought the direction he was going, we were going, it would crash against me even harder. I was grateful for that insight resurfacing in me right when I needed it most. It helped.

An insight I later gleaned of what may have happened in him to catalyze his shutting down is that before he met me he hadn't wanted to be in a relationship. I remembered that his best friend, Bibi, had told me he had said that. Emanuele had a lot of fear and well hidden insecurities. Before meeting me he had decided he wanted to remain alone. But then when he met and fell in love with me it created a lot of inner conflict for him.

When we met I was already engaging and going really deep into my explorations of self, which is what he loved about me and it inspired him. He was exploring himself too, but, as can happen in many, he reached a point where going deeper scared him so he avoided it and numbed it with the drugs and alcohol. He also had a lot of unresolved issues both with his ex-girlfriend and his mother. To heal and become whole we have to engage our shadows and the emotional pains we hold deep within. Sometimes we can go so far but then we get stuck and then we sabotage ourselves and our relationships.

I knew he loved me beyond a doubt, but that's what can happen when we have so much unresolved hidden subconscious gunk, and we don't know how to address and talk about it. Once we get triggered in one of these buried emotional landmines, it can get so inflamed so fast that we go into fight, flight, or freeze mode and our heart shuts down. Our limbic system takes over and our heart and higher reasoning falter. This is where far too many relationships fall apart. We shut down and put up numbing walls that appear to protect us, but they actually only disconnect us more. I sense something like this happened for him.

Any journey of love will lead us to this kind of conflict because in order to love we need to heal what separates us from it. Everything that is buried will inevitably come up or blow up in our faces when we are in love. We need to know this so we can navigate these emotional storms, not buy into the fear, and come out intact, even healed, on the other side. Due to whatever unresolved past traumas he had experienced, love clearly no longer felt like a safe place to him. The vulnerability needed to love and be loved felt too dangerous, so he shut down. I had glimpses of these insights then, but I, too, still had so many subconscious undercurrents that made it hard for me to stay grounded in that understanding. As I healed in the coming years it all became clearer.

When you think of it, where were we ever taught to navigate emotional pain? Where were we given tools to understand and navigate the complex worlds within us? Nowhere. So is it any wonder we are ruled by our fears, rather than our hearts? The subconscious triggers that shut us down actually have the potential of being portals where we can meet and understand ourselves and each other more. Triggers can actually deepen the love and care we have for each other when we use them with awareness. We need to learn to just talk when we want to withdraw and run, and reveal ourselves when we want to attack. It is really that simple. But that takes work and needing to endure discomfort at times as we go beyond our comfort zone with eachother.

Emanuele didn't have the inner resources to understand why he was feeling what he was feeling, and the drugs and alcohol certainly didn't help at all either, so he made the most base interpretation and followed that. That's what we do. Our main priority is to feel safe, and shutting down feels safe, so we don't question it further. The only way though to a truly deep connection is absolute vulnerability, but for the most part we meet through our protective patterns that make vulnerability impossible, so love fades. Love cannot grow in the shallows.

I was working hard on myself, trying to understand and let go. I was in a lot of pain, doing my best to reach for the bigger picture and a higher perspective so I could move on and also hold space for him to be him, even if that meant separation.

About a week before he went away, I had befriended a wild puppy who's mother had her pups close to our cabin. He was the cutest little guy and after just a few days he loved me so much and I certainly loved him too. Emanuele wasn't as warm to him as I was, but I didn't care, this puppy became a lifeline of love and joy for me.

While Emanuele was away the puppy, who I called Puppy as his name, and I bonded even more, I even had let him sleep with me. What a Godsend this this little beauty was. So much love and sweetness touching and nourishing my broken heart.

When Emanuele came back from his training he was even more distant, and one night he said to me, with a cold heart, that he didn't even miss me. Wow! That hurt.

Of course not, I thought to myself, *he had already shut his heart down and was comfortable and safe in his protective patterning, so why would he miss me?* I almost had to laugh inside at the parody of it all.

I started sleeping at Loreene's that night. It was just too much. I wasn't going to put myself through the same torture as the first time around. I was getting stronger.

Most of my clothing and stuff was still in our bungalow, and Puppy was still with his mama and siblings near our bungalow so I would go play with him during the day and get my things as I needed them.

He barely acknowledged me until about a week after I left the bungalow, when one day he actually started talking to me nicely again. What that meant I didn't know, but my heart was hopeful, but also protecting itself. We had a casual conversation, then I went back to Loreene's. The next day after that he was nice again, reaching out. Then again. I started feeling hope grow and that the Emanuele I once knew was again coming through.

Then one morning he asked me if I wanted join him for a mushroom omelet, I thought that was peculiar, I had never seen omelets on the menu. I commented that to him and he laughed saying it's a magic mushroom omelet. I had heard that mushrooms were the love drug, that it deepens and awakens love and affectionate feelings. I was hesitant, but a part of me thought, maybe since it seems his heart is opening again, taking them with him will reawaken and remind him of his love for me our love for each other. God Bless. I was so naïve and vulnerable I would have done almost anything to get us back together now that I was feeling his old self emerging again. I said okay. He told Pan and she made the omelets for us. It tasted good. I loved the flavor of mushrooms. I had absolutely no idea what to expect.

Shortly thereafter I had a bit of a tummy ache and then my senses started feeling weird. The Nature around me became brighter and more beautiful. Emanuele was close by, but no affection came from him at all. So I went and sat on the beach alone for a while.

While I was sitting there I had this sensation of looking out of my eyes as if they were windows in a house, feeling separate from my body. It was an interesting feeling, but a bit freaky. I started thinking things like life is an illusion, nothing is real, stuff like that. Then I started feeling not so well so I went back to our bungalow and laid down. That was at maybe 11 in the morning.

I blacked out and didn't come to until 6:30 p.m. I was so disoriented. Something happened that pushed my brain over its natural threshold. I felt absolutely shattered inside and it scared me. There is a word I didn't know then, but describes what happened: "dissociation." I felt completely scrambled. For the next few days all I kept saying is life is a trip in a kind of manic way. There was a layer to this experience that I felt had opened my awareness to an aspect of reality of life; that we were all caught up in beliefs and ideas cause us to create so much nonsense in our lives. It felt like Neo waking up from the Matrix and seeing behind the programs we believe about life because that's what we were taught, and we're not supposed to question what we are taught. My perceptions sharpened immensely. I was feeling everything, each moment was so intense, in Ultra High Definition, it was almost unbearable. I was completely ungrounded. I had no idea how to understand what I was feeling to navigate it better. It was so far out from anything I had ever experienced before.

Once in my punk phase, I had tried acid, it was called a purple mike, and I had a really bad trip. I was super paranoid that everyone hated me. I felt like that for several hours and then it finally wore off. I never did any heavy drugs again! After that I had just drank more alcohol and sometimes took caffeine pills, like speed, to feel a buzz when hanging out with my street friends. This experience felt a bit similar but far more terrifying.

This mushroom experience felt so much more overwhelming, the intense sensations never went away in the days that followed.

Even without the mushrooms, so much had already changed in me that it would have been a challenge reintegrating myself back with my life and family. This threw over the top, the effect of the mushrooms made it even harder to be alive really. My little Puppy gave me love through it all which helped me so much.

Emanuele was distant again after that experience. A few days later I decided it was enough and was time to go back to Switzerland. Even in the state I was in, I knew I couldn't stay any longer. I had no idea what I would do or where I would stay, I just knew I had to go.

It was approaching May, when the Hotels in Tessin would be hiring for the coming season. I hoped I would be able to find work and a new place to live quickly when I got there.

I took a motorcycle taxi to Tongsala to change my departure date the same day I made the decision to go. I would now leave in four days, a month earlier then planned.

I stayed with Loreene my last days. She was very supportive and gave me counsel many times trying to help me land in myself again before going.

I would visit Puppy every day, he would never venture beyond the bungalow, I truly don't know what I would have done without the love exchanged with that precious being. My eyes water as I share this. Our pets and how they love us. It's amazing.

I reflected on my experiences; I had been away for six months on this epic journey that totally changed my life and my understanding of myself in many amazing and wonderful ways, before this bad mushroom trip. Now after that experience I felt so scrambled and even more confused about it all. It all felt like a dream.

I was nervous going back and I was so scared by how I was feeling still since the mushrooms. Manic and fragmented are the best words I can use to describe how I felt. I was told the effects of the mushrooms would wear off by the time I got back. I sure hoped it would be so.

The day I had to leave was a traumatic one. I got up early to finish packing and get ready to go. Normally Puppy always stayed back at the bungalow when I would go to Loreenes, this morning though he followed me. It was so sweet, it was almost as if he knew I was leaving. He was following me down the path, I felt so joyful about that fact when all of a sudden I heard him yelp with great pain. As I turned around I saw the bully dog of the area had grabbed him by the neck and was shaking him wildly. I screamed and charged at the dog and he finally dropped my Puppy and ran away.

My little guy was still yelping, turning in circles in panic and fear that when I reached to hold him he bit my right thumb quite deeply. My poor little guy. I reached for him again and this time he let me pick him up. He was shaking. My heart broke. And now I had to leave him in this state. I didn't know what to do, and my thumb was bleeding strongly.

I brought him over to Loreene and asked her to watch him, letting her know that I had to get to the medical clinic to clean my wound and get a tetanus shot before going.

Pan drove me on her motorcycle as quickly as possible to the clinic in Tongsala. They saw me right away and gave me a few stitches, wrapped me up, gave the tetanus shot and off we went back to Seaview.

Emanuele was really indifferent and couldn't care less about the puppy. I had asked him to take care of him when I left, he refused. I asked Loreene if she would keep him for me and she thankfully agreed.

I felt so terrible leaving him. My heart still sinks a little when I think of my little sweetie. I quickly got my things together and then got a ride in the truck back to Tongsala to catch the ferry back to Surrathani where I would then catch the train back to Bangkok.

What an emotional final day there. I couldn't get the image of Puppy out of my head when he was in the dogs mouth and his yelping and turning in circles in so much pain and confusion. It just replayed itself in my mind over and over again.

In some ways years later, I saw how the mirror reflection of his outer expression was reflecting how I had actually felt inside. He had lost all orientation in those moments, just as I had. I hoped and trusted he would be ok.

Back in Bangkok I ran into Fred gain. That was nice. It was helpful seeing him and talking with him. I shared what happened and he supported, counselled, and consoled me. He encouraged me to trust that I would find my way, that I am strong and capable. His words helped. We exchanged addresses to keep in touch.

On my last day I ate my favourite Cashew Chicken and I bought myself some new tops and sarongs to bring back with me and then off I went, this time with apprehension and fear in my heart about returning and what would come next. I only had a few hundred Swiss Frank's to live on, I needed to find work fast, but was also questioning my capacity to work considering the inner state I was in. I decided to just trust it would all work out as it always had until then.

My flight back to Switzerland was through Romania again. This time there was a longer stop over where the airlines paid for a hotel. That was so amazing! I was able to have my first hot bath in months, and oh, did I relish every second! Also sleeping in a really nice bed rather than the thin mattresses on hard surfaces as I had gotten used to was deluxe! After my relaxing bath and nap I went downstairs to the restaurant for lunch.

The hotel was built on a lake side with a stunning view. The architecture was breathtaking; it felt like I was in a castle. What a perfect bridge and interlude to my journey back to Switzerland. So much had happened in those past months, so much to sort through and integrate. I was so grateful to be there.

Many of the others who were brought to the Hotel with me decided to go into town, I was so enamored with the hotel and lake that I decided to stay and enjoy every minute of it and spent some time journaling. It was nice for me to just be at the hotel and hang out. I really needed the pause. It couldn't have been more perfect!

After a great night's sleep I went down for breakfast with the other passengers then we were picked up and brought back to the airport. Off I went again into the great unknown!

6

CRASH LANDING

Distant memories of a past long forgotten,
almost haunting.
So many unworked through experiences and memories,
so much left to be realized, digested before I can feel whole.
At the moment my life before 20 feels like a void,
though I do have some vague memories to fill it,
it doesn't feel real and I have a difficult time talking about it
or feeling it. Until I come to terms with my past and
piece the pieces together
I will feel this uneasiness.
Only then can I release this knot in my stomach and mind
and move on.
- Journal Entry, Thailand, November 4, 1992. 21 years of age.

When I landed back in Switzerland I felt so disoriented. Everything was so intense and felt foreign to me. I was still tripping out, perhaps even more so because of the culture shock. In Thailand because of the different rhythm of living it didn't feel quite so unsettling and scary, but being back in the western world was a whole different frequency to adjust to. I, my awareness, and biology had been forever changed by the experience with the mushrooms.

When I returned to Locarno I had nowhere to go so, I called an acquaintance who I knew had a bed and breakfast.

I asked him if I could temporarily rent a room until I figured out what I was going to do. He was a nice guy; I wish I could remember his name to honor his kindness here.

I felt so odd and out of place -- a complete stranger to myself. It's hard to describe the sensations I experienced of dissociation from all that I had known before. It was all foreign to me. It was like my whole life had been shattered into pieces, my memories totally fragmented. I could see the pieces but not integrate them as a whole. Before 20, I had virtually no memories of my life before. I shared a bit of my confusion with him when we met for lunch the following day, in what used to be my favorite restaurant. He was sympathetic and said not to worry, things will work out, that I was a good person and that I can stay as long as I needed. He even gave me a discounted rate.

I remembered someone had mentioned to me once that often when people live in places like Nepal and Asia for an extended time, when they come home they experience a kind of culture shock. That insight matched my experience when I had arrived. I decided that must be a part of what I was experiencing, so that was the explanation with which I chose to navigate. It gave me some peace and helped me feel less crazy.

I was still coming off the effects of the mushrooms, at least I hoped I was. I really hoped these sensations would finally stop.

It was just a week ago that I was on the island with Puppy and Loreene. It felt like a dream. Now I was back in Locarno and I felt so out of place. What would I do? I had no home, no work, and was running out of money fast. I remembered the Yoga Loreene taught me and started doing that in the mornings and at night to ground me. It helped a lot.

It's such a different rhythm when you are travelling. Everything is always new and fresh. There are no routines, it's intense, your senses are heightened because you are more fully engaged in the moment. You have to be. Also people are not as guarded. You can easily enter into deep and meaningful conversations, and friendships grow strong fast.

Back in Switzerland and the West in general, I realized it was very different. I became aware that everything is based in routine, which numbs our senses and I felt people were not so open and transparent as I had experienced traveling. My senses were the most heightened they had ever been; now, everything around me, and everyone, felt dead, no energy or vitality, they all felt like robots.

That's what it felt like, and it freaked me out. Who was I in this world? I didn't know anymore. The only constant in me was my love and connection to Nature, so I spent as much time by the lake or in the forest as possible.

I slept a lot the next days. Feeling so overwhelmed and afraid to go out among the masses, I would bee-line it to the lake and just sit there, letting myself be lulled by the gentle waters.

It was so strange, I had no fear in Asia anymore, I had felt incredibly confident and I was so eager to engage and meet people, but now here in Locarno I experienced fear verging on paranoia. I found people's energies and personalities really painful to my body. I could feel all the buried and suppressed feelings they carried and saw through the masks they put on to cover them. I didn't feel safe because everyone felt like a liar, they felt false.

I experienced time like in the movies, when they slow everything down to intensify the moment. I lived like that every second, every day. It was maddening. My only place of refuge from those feelings was in Nature. In Nature the intensity felt beautiful and invigorating, I felt at ease and at felt at home. Among people, though, it felt like hell. What was at first only fear, began to grow into anxiety, depression and paranoia.

One day I went to visit Emanuele's parents, all my belongings were stored in their basement storage locker. His mother made us lunch and when it was approaching time for me to leave they invited me to stay with them until I found a new job and apartment. Since I was running out of money I accepted their offer, though it felt a bit uncomfortable. Regardless, I was very grateful for their kindness.

I moved back in with them and stayed in Emanuele's room. To my brain, it was like another drug trip. All the beautiful memories that room had once held of love and friendship, now there was nothing. It felt empty and dark. It was hard to be there, but on another level it was good for me to be there because it helped me ground and integrate some of the fragments of my past. When I went to the basement one day where I had stored my things, I went into shock. I looked at my pictures of me, my belongings, and had no feeling of connection to them whatsoever.

I knew logically they were my things, but I had no feelings or memories associated with them. It was all blank. Dissociative Amnesia, I found out later, is the term to describe what I was experiencing. I wanted to panic and freak out, but somehow I knew if I gave in to the panic completely I would lose myself totally. So I took deep breaths and reminded myself I am okay, it's just culture shock, it will pass.

I had learned in my life how to create a façade so I could hide my feelings when I needed to feel safe and to survive, so I accessed that part of me. I was afraid if anyone caught on to what was happening in me they would send me to the psych ward or something. I straightened myself up, dried my tears, kept breathing, and I went back to my room where I continued crying until I fell asleep, not letting anything on that something was wrong.

Of course the people around me would have seen an extreme difference in my mannerisms but I tried to meet the world as if there was nothing wrong with me. When I was alone though, I let myself feel everything.

Always I felt best when I was in Nature so I continued to go to my forest or to the lake every day. That was my one source of sanity and solace. There is no way I would have made it through this time without Nature. Absolutely no way. I could be in a manic place and I would go there and be soothed. It would all melt away in Nature.

I had a tree in this tree in a beautiful grove that became like my temple or altar. It was my tree for praying, crying, and just being. I am so grateful that I have had this connection to Nature all my life, that I never forgot it, even when everything else fell away.

As I wrote in the introduction here, "Nature saved my life." This is the experience to which I was referring.

I fortunately found a job and an apartment that week. The interview was hard. I felt completely opposite to who I was claiming to be, who I had been before all this happened. I had to pretend.

Putting on appearances, I seemed like a solid person, which got me both the job and the apartment. But how was I going to maintain it at work? I was so fragile, it didn't take much to make me cry, and I was constantly overwhelmed by my senses picking up every subtlety around me. My survival depended on my being able to earn money so I knew I had to muster up every strength I had to make it work.

Bibi helped me move into my new place. It was an overwhelming process, getting everything together to bring to my new home. It was a beautiful old building up a mountainside, Via San Carlo 76. It was a large space with a nice balcony, and, one of my favorite things, a church nearby, that rang its bells every day, every hour. It was perfect!

Once we got everything in Bibi left right away. I had invited her to stay a bit but she said she had to get home.

Now, I was alone in my new home. My body had been shaking the whole time we were moving things in. As soon as she walked out the door and I closed it behind her, I experienced a total breakdown.

I curled up in a ball in the bathroom and just wailed and cried for I don't know how long. Then, still shaking to the bone, I washed my face with cold water. Tried to affirm to myself I would be okay. I couldn't look at myself in the mirror though, it felt weird that I had a body, I felt totally dissociated from my body, even looking at it. I was falling apart. My body was ice cold all the time. My feet felt like they were frozen. I climbed into bed upon my mattress on the floor, I had no furniture yet, and fell asleep, praying for help and crying. I was so far away from who I had once been. I felt so scared, lost, and alone.

I went to see Brigitte for the first time since my return at her store the next day. She saw right away something was wrong with me. I shared everything. She was so present and loving. She and her husband Peter set to work on me to get me back in my body. He did three-to-four-hour psycho-therapeutic bodywork sessions on me for many weeks, twice a week. I had no idea what that was but I was grateful for all the love and support they offered me.

The first session blew me away. As he was massaging me, my neurosis was looping as always, then he applied deep pressure to a point and it was like I went through a door in me and all of a sudden I was screaming, wailing in absolute anguish.

It wasn't a thought or conscious memory that caused that reaction in me, so it was confusing, but I couldn't stop.

What he later told me had happened was that he had catalyzed the release of a trauma charge in my body. He came to my side and held me and said "I don't know who did this to you, but someone hurt you really badly a long time ago." I just sobbed and cried so deeply for so long; there was an endless well of tears and sadness in me. When the sobs finally slowed down and subsided, he did a bit of work on my neck and feet that soothed me and then the session was over.

When I got up I asked him, "What happened? Where did that come from?" He explained to me how we store unhealed traumas in our bodies. That the technique he practices helps to release those emotions from the body. It helps to unload the stress in the nervous system that the stored traumas create, which then enables the body and mind to finally heal.

Wow! It was incredible. I did feel a bit lighter then when I had arrived, a little more like me again. Through his work, after a few sessions I started regaining memories. In one of my journal writings I described it as feeling like movie scenes flashing before me, as how some have described what happens when we die. At times that became overwhelming too, but at least I was remembering.

Brigitte worked with me as well through the coming months, doing Energy Healing, Bach Flowers, Aromatherapy, Crystal Healings and she taught me a traditional form of Tarot that you won't find in any book used for personal healing, that had been passed down for generations. She taught me this as a way to connect to my soul and heal.

They never charged me a penny and worked on me for the next four months non-stop. I wouldn't be here today without them. I still had my sensitivity, that never went away, but I was less loaded emotionally, which enabled me to navigate my new sensitivity better and reduced the anxiety and paranoia I had previously been experiencing.

In those months I often called Iona, my Spiritual Mentor from the Crystal store in Toronto, regularly. I was so grateful to have her in my life.

One time I phoned her from the phone booth at the end of my street crying hysterically when I first moved in. I was telling her how confused I was and all the stuff I was feeling. Her response was "Good! That's great!"

I paused for a moment in shock. *"What do you mean good? I feel awful."* I said. She told me it was good because it meant things were happening and changing in me for healing. That confusion is a good sign that patterns, thoughts and awareness are being shifted.

Hmmm, I thought to myself. It kind of made sense to me once she explained that. From that moment I chose to use that way of seeing things whenever I felt overwhelmed. It really helped me navigate through those emotional spaces better. When I chose that way of perceiving my experience it was easier for me to move forward and allow the sorting and growth process to happen in me naturally.

I started trusting the process and also trusting that I would come out the other end. Taking the view of my experience as being a combination of culture shock and spiritual awakening gave me a kind of map or foundation to frame my experience in a way that was less scary and where I felt I had the power of choice to learn to direct my emotions rather than be high-jacked and run by them. It was hard work, let me tell you. Sometimes my emotions felt like a stampede of a thousand horses pulling me toward a cliff that I had to reign in to keep myself going and growing.

One night after a healing session something Peter said to me affirmed the insight Iona gave me that day on the phone. Apparently in Hebrew there are two words, Ben and Benah, that describe the process of Spiritual Awakening.

In the state of Ben, a tree is a tree, a mountain is a mountain, an ocean is an ocean. In the state of Benah also a tree is a tree and a mountain is a mountain and an ocean is an ocean.

However, in the journey between those two states of awareness, from Ben to Benah, a tree is not a tree and a mountain is not a mountain, it all gets mixed up and confused. Up is down, down is up, nothing is what it once was and we are left to sort it out and bring new awareness and order to our understanding of life and our place in this world.

That metaphor became a stronghold for me, gave me a way to frame my experience that I reconnected to many times over the coming years as I continued to heal and regain my memories. I actually think that understanding saved me as well. It helped rebuilt and restored my mind each time I remembered and applied that awareness to whatever I was going through.

One night after a session Peter took me for a walk. We climbed a small escarpment to where there was a bench where we could sit and enjoy the view over Locarno. He sat to my right and while looking ahead he said to me, "I have only known a few people in my life that reached the living awareness and experience of time and the level of sensitivity that has awakened in you. There are people in Monasteries and Mystery Schools all around the world learning and studying to prepare for this sensitivity when it awakens in them, so they have the knowledge to navigate it when that time comes.

With you, he said, the process has happened in reverse. You have been opened up and awakened first. So your job now is to gather the knowledge and information you need to anchor and ground this experience so that it doesn't tear you apart." As he looked at me deeply, I felt the sincerity and truth in his words and thanked him.

I told him that sometimes I felt like I was going crazy. He chuckled and said, "As long as you are capable of questioning yourself about being crazy, you are not." That made me laugh, for what may have been the first time in a long time. We then sat in silence for a few more moments while I absorbed everything he had just said. It calmed my mind and gave me another new reference point to understand and navigate all I was experiencing. He validated that not only was I experiencing a culture shock, I was also experiencing a deep spiritual awakening.

God Bless him. In this moment as I revisit and write this, my heart is so deep and full of gratitude for him. I don't know how I would have made it through without his wise guidance.

Both he, Brigitte and my forest were my lifeline those months. I also found another crystal store in Old Locarno called Amethyst where I purchased a lot of healing crystals and spent time with the woman who owned it, too.

I continued with my Yoga every morning and for the first time in my life I kept my apartment immaculate. Anything out of place stressed me out. I learned later that wasn't an uncommon reality with PTSD. I continued to spend all my spare time in Nature and learning the pendulum, tarot, and crystal healing.

Another time, when I called Iona she told me I should eat meat. I was shocked again! I had been a vegetarian for several years and the thought of eating meat horrified me. She told me that sometimes eating meat can help ground our nervous system and balance our brain chemistry because of the protein when we are undergoing acute stress. I listened but had no intention of following that advice until....

One day I was receiving another session with Peter. It was incredible how effective this form of bodywork was to access and free trauma charges in my body, how it could quiet my mind, too, when I was otherwise still in a sea of neurosis most of the time.

I had just experienced another emotional release and suddenly I found myself craving a burger. *What!!!* I thought *Impossible!*

I was absolutely stunned by that, but I could not deny my body had just grown fangs and wanted meat!

The conundrum that created in me in that moment was actually quite funny. I can't help chuckling as I write this.

At the end of the session I cautiously ventured to share this with Peter. He responded, "Well, let's get you a burger, then!!" He then brought me to this outdoor burger place by the river, and I tell ya, nothing ever tasted so good to my body then that burger in that moment! My body was in bliss! I couldn't believe it, but it was true! It was then that I decided to listen to my body rather than force a certain diet on it. I decided that whenever my body wanted meat I would feed it that.

It did make a difference, I did become more grounded as Iona had said I would, and my mind did become stronger, clearer than it had been in a long, long time.

Working was really hard though. It was a constant challenge to be present and do what I was hired to do. A few times a day, pretty much every day, I had to retreat to the bathroom to have a cry, but nonetheless, I would warrior it through the day.

At home I would write in my journal to try to move some of what I was feeling out of my body and mind to the paper. It helped a lot. I would also cry every night. Literally.

One night while I was crying, huddled in my new little sofa chair, there was a gentle knock on my door. I dried my tears and opened it. There stood my neighbor from above my apartment with a white rose in his hand. He gently asked me if I was okay. That he always heard me crying, and that if I needed a friend and someone to talk to he was there for me.

I cried again and thanked him. I'm actually crying right now as I remember and write this. The kindness of strangers. It's so beautiful and I am so grateful again for his kind gesture. We ended up becoming friends and that friendship helped me come more out of myself.

I had met many other people as well, and many other experiences that brought me little bits of healing too, as I moved forward, though those shared here were the most poignant.

In those months I had still hoped to hear from Emanuele. I knew when he had come back in June. I had hoped he would come see me right away when he arrived. Alas he did not. It was so hard to let him go from my heart. No one had ever touched it deeper, which is why I clung to the memories so tightly.

When He finally came by to see me in August I had already healed a lot and was not clinging as much. He apologized again, said he didn't know what had happened to him, that it wasn't anything wrong with me. He said that he was stopping drinking and drugs.

I had yearned the whole summer long, waiting for him to come see me, but now that he was there it was a peculiar feeling in me, no words to describe. I had written him a letter that summer angry at him and telling him what state my life was in because of him, trying to understand the pain and confusion I was going through.

I was clearly feeling much better after all the healing work by the time he finally came. I was definitely much stronger. He commented about the letter and said to me that I looked fine to him, that it musn't have been as bad as I wrote. I was stunned by that insensitive and hurtful comment. I responded, *"Oh yes it was, and worse. I am healing now though and had a lot of love and support from Brigitte and Peter."*

He wasn't very interested in any of the spiritual insights or understandings, he had shut that part of him down. He said the spiritual path only creates confusion.

I agreed with him on that and said *" yes, temporarily, because it shakes things up, but if you stick with it you come out the other end stronger, more aware, and life becomes more fulfilling. "* He didn't really hear me. We chatted superficially a bit more and then he left.

Well, at least there was some form of closure. Quite anti-climactic really. I had somehow anticipated something else. I had still had a hidden hope that he would finally see and remember me and hoped he would come around, but I could clearly see that because he shut down that vital part of him there was no meeting place for us anymore. I felt a bit sad about that because he had once had so much joy in the journey. Now he felt dulled to how I once knew him. That's what happens when we go numb, our overall vitality gets diminished because we can't isolate what we numb down. It eventually spreads through our whole being, like a slow fog taking over so we don't notice and don't remember how life felt before we shut down. In spite of the sadness I felt, I also felt a relief. Now I could finally start fully letting go.

I made it through work to the end of August, thank God! What a feat that was! I was actually under contract until November, but they didn't want me there anymore, which I understood, they couldn't understand me and found me too emotional, which I was, so they laid me off. This fortunately enabled me to get unemployment until December. That was a relief.

A few months before, Brigitte had told me about this retreat center in the mountains of Intragnia, a neighboring town to Locarno.

One day once I stopped working, an inner nudge guided me to ask her if she thought I might be able to go up there to continue my healing. She told me to write them a letter about my situation. She would get it to him, then the Retreat Center owner would contact me if I qualify to go. Being immersed in Nature sounded like the perfect medicine for me, I hoped he would accept me there. I wrote the letter and waited.

Brigitte heard from him a few days later and he told her I was welcome to go there anytime.

I packed some things right away and made my way to Intragnia; it was a long and beautiful mountain hike to get there. I felt my heart happy and growing as I trekked up that mountainside. It was so beautiful!

What a magical paradise it was! My healing process that they "prescribed" for me was chopping wood, tending to the garden, and cooking for the people who were staying there. They also did a bit of energy work on me, ear candling, and singing mantras, but mostly those were my tasks to ground me back in my body. That was perfect because Nature was my sanctuary and I have always loved cooking for other people. That was definitely the best medicine for me.

About two weeks into my stay a man came to visit. He was a friend of a friend of one of the facilitators there. We clicked. It was the first time I felt my heart open in trust in a long time. I was still dealing with being overly sensitized and had a hard time trusting people, but he had a really clear heart, more than most. His name was Michael Kern. He told me of a shaman from Peru that he was going to a retreat with at a Spiritual Centre in Brienze, called Schweibenalp. I said I'd love to go but my finances were very limited. He generously offered to pay for me and for my transportation there. Another blessing.

I could feel Michael was developing romantic feelings for me though, but I knew I couldn't go there. I clarified this before accepting his offer. He was very gracious and kind, totally accepting where I was at.

I had an inner resonant tug when he mentioned the elder the first time in an earlier conversation, so it was magic that this unfolded this way. My inner nudges were returning and I was starting to trust them again. That felt good.

A few days later we headed off. The place was like a spiritual ashram. Everyone was wearing saris and hippie-style clothing, like in Nepal. I felt comfortable and at ease, which was incredible considering where I had been all those months before. I started feeling more like who I was before the shock and trauma took me over.

I saw more clearly that what had changed about me most with everything that had happened, is that I had become more withheld in myself, I was not as eagerly open and buoyant like I used to be. I realized I missed that part of me, but understood I had been, and still was somewhat, stuck in hypervigilance, waiting for bad things to happen at any time. So, withholding myself was a kind of self-preservation and protection mode that I had gone into when I returned from Asia except with people I knew and trusted.

I was staying in a dorm room with two other women. I was a bit nervous about being so close with them but I opened up more and more as the retreat progressed. They were really nice. One of them taught me a healing Mantra which I did use a lot in the years to come.

All the participants for the retreat met the first night in the big hall space. I wanted to sit right at the front, so I did. The shaman, was sitting on his blanket with his medicine altar in front of him. He was burning a beautiful sweet-smelling wood on a piece of incense coal on a shell. Once everyone was there he did an opening prayer and started teaching about shamanism; I felt really connected. I did my first sweat lodge there too. I had no idea what to expect.

The Sweat Lodge is practiced as a way to symbolically return to the womb for healing and guidance. We were all to go in naked, as we had come out of our mother's womb. I wrapped myself in a towel though, I was not very comfortable with that. Once inside when it was dark I loosened the towel since no one could see me.

The hot stones, Grandmothers and Grandfathers, were brought in to the center pit of the sweat lodge. I was nervous. The lady beside me felt that and held my hand, she affirmed to me that I will be fine. She even held my hand for a while.

The opening was closed and Inti started pouring the water on the rocks praying. He passed around a feather each of us could hold when it came around the circle to us when we could then speak our prayers and gratitude.

We learned healing chants and songs. It got so hot that when I breathed in, it felt like my nose and mouth were on fire. It was so hard to breathe. He told us to let the heat in, to not resist it, to keep breathing and it would subside, but if it got too much we can briefly put our head close to the ground where it was cooler. I had to do that once but then wanted to stay upright the rest of the time. It took a lot of mind power to do that, but I did and it was powerful.

I prayed for my family, for healing of everyone, healing for me, and particularly with my mother. I cried so deeply over the sadness of the deterioration of my relationship with her. I also gave gratitude for the many graces and blessings I had received. That is one aspect that I really love about Native wisdoms and teachings. The focus on gratitude.

When the sweat lodge ceremony was complete we all went out into the snow. I laid down in it with my towel around me, I was shy about my body, always had been. It felt beautiful rolling in the freezing snow with my body being so cooking hot. I was so hot I was steaming!

I hugged a tree for a few minutes, giving gratitude again for the blessing of being there until we were called to go back to the building and get ready for a feast.

The day after, when I was feeling some overwhelm rising in me, I went and sat in the shell of the sweat lodge for a while. I cried and prayed. Then I felt a song rhythm come over me, then the sounds to that rhythm, and I started singing. I received my first soul song. It felt really beautiful and I just kept singing, wanting to imprint it in me so I wouldn't forget it.

One of the coordinators, Michelle, came and sat with me for a bit. I had shared some of what I was going through and she gave me a hug. She had a very loving and nurturing way about her. I felt safe in her presence and let myself cry as she held me. A lot of healing and learning happened for me at this magical place.

We were there for five days. I could feel Michael's attraction growing for me. I actually felt attracted to him too, but I was still too broken to allow anything to happen. He remained kind about it, but I could see he felt a bit hurt that I wouldn't let myself go there. I just couldn't. I thanked him when it came time to leave and we exchanged information to connect again sometime down the road.

I went back to the retreat centre in Intrgnia and stayed there until October. During all the past months I had kept in contact with Fred from Thailand. He was always sending me cards with nice pictures and inspirational quotes. I was still in Intragnia when we talked on the phone one day. He suggested that I should go back to Thailand. He offered to pick me up and bring me to a place I could stay if I decided to. I told him I had to watch my money; that I wanted to but didn't think I could.

The next thing he said, quoting a quote he had sent to me earlier that summer, hit me in the gut: "What would you rather have? A breach of pocket or a breach of life?" I had read it before but it didn't have the same impact as that day. So I said, "Let me see what I can do." I started feeling that fire of urgency in my gut again like that morning of the World Healing Meditation. I decided to trust it and do what I could to make it happen.

I went back to my apartment, sold a bunch of my clothes and belongings. I also made a bunch of jewelry to sell to Brigitte, Serge and to the lady from the Amethyst store. Between them all they bought everything.

I needed to get enough money together to pay for my apartment while I was away and a bit of spending money, I figured I could probably get a job teaching English in Bangkok like Fred suggested. It sounded crazy and risky, but somehow that's what I needed, I just knew it. I needed to get into the spontaneous flow of life again. By the time I finished selling everything I could I had made good money, more than enough. Yes! I was ready.

An acquaintance I had met with Emanuele, Petra, who owned the travel agency where we had bought our tickets the last time, found me a good flight. I booked it and was off back to Thailand the next week. I felt excited and hoped to be able to piece some missing pieces from my experience together to heal the trauma residues. I felt alive, with joy sparkling in my heart again. It sure felt good!

7

BACK IN THE FLOW

Great Spirit, Father Sky, whose voice I hear in the wind.
Ancient Tree Spirits,
who share of their wisdom, guiding and soothing.
Earth Mother,
who touches me with the music of her ever-flowing waters,
whose breath gives me life.
Help and guide me to walk the paths of my life with Beauty,
Strength, and Wisdom,
that I may learn the lessons of my days,
and hear and follow the intuition of my inner voice. To not be
blinded by the false voices of fear, doubt, and indecision.
To live honestly, compassionately, and harmoniously, in peace
with myself and surroundings.
Give me strength to accept and learn from my greatest teachers,
pain and ignorance,
that I may see the wisdom they offer.
I ask for guidance and protection on my journey, that I may
learn the lessons of my experiences fully and clearly.
To reach the quiet place of acceptance and
Unconditional Love within my Being,
breaking free from this dizzying circle of conflict
and chaos that has been binding me.
That I may put aside my ego and false pride to
forgive my "enemies" and harvest the gifts
that my experiences with them offer.

To be able to Love, Nourish, and Heal myself,
my family and my Brothers and Sisters.
That the Love of Mother Earth nourish, teach and sustain me.
May all the powers of all Directions;
South, Sacred Mouse, teacher of Innocence and Trust.
West, home of the Bear, place of Intuition and looking within.
North, home of the Buffalo, place of great Wisdom and
Knowledge, and East, home of the Eagle
that flies free of man's restrictions,
place of Illumination, Visionary Truth and experience,
Great Spirit, Mother Earth, Father Sky, Arraiah,
please guide and keep me.
I give thanks for my Bounty.
Blessed Be. HO!
- Journal Entry, April 1992, Locarno, Switzerland, 22 years of age.

F red picked me up at the airport and brought me to a
place called the Peachy Guest House. It was a nice big
place, clean, much nicer than the one Emanuele and I
stayed at. There were real toilets, not just a hole in the ground
with a ceramic frame to squat on like at Guest House 59 where
you had to fill a bucket of water to flush your "stuff" down
the pipe. What a treat that was!

Fred took me out for dinner and introduced me to many
of his friends. I felt so good being back in Thailand, better
than I had felt in all the time I was in Switzerland.

I was still learning to navigate my senses being so sensitive,
but somehow it wasn't as difficult nor as intense there, as I
had experienced the last months. Life in Bangkok was bustling
and always moving, like a strong and steady current in a river.
My brain actually seemed to feel more comfortable with the
constant change and stimulation of adventure,. It's like to be
there and navigate my sensitivity was useful to being in the
moment, versus in Switzerland the robotic feeling of life their
felt like it was on repeat, no vitality, no sense of adventure
which drove me to feel so uncomfortable and out of place.

I found that interesting, it was opposite of what I would have imagined based on how overwhelmed I was in Switzerland by what seemed like over stimulation at the time.

Upon reflecting I realized it was the frequency of life and consciousness that was different in Asia in general. It's a completely other rhythm and lifestyle. I felt so much more at home both in the culture and with the people of Thailand and the rhythm of being a traveler then being stuck living the same old routines in the West. Life in Thailand was really based on living in the present, in the now, which naturally demands our senses to be very sharp and alert.

No wonder I was always fascinated with Gypsies when I was younger I thought to myself! I was a gypsy at heart! I had never felt at home anywhere as I did there. I felt I belonged 100% ...that felt really nice.

Every day I sang the healing songs that I learned at the Shamanic Retreat in Switzerland as a way to connect and ground. One day a young woman approached me after hearing me sing in the communal shower and wanted to learn the songs. I was happy to share them. Her name was Steffi.

She was an artist and made some of the most beautiful pastel drawings I had ever seen. She also wove bracelets and other things that were so beautiful and unique. I asked her to teach me, so she did. A beautiful friendship developed between us. Once I learned from her I loved getting absorbed in the weaving, it was like a meditation for me. It relaxed me a lot.

I reconnected and spent some time with Chad too, the fellow that made the moccasins and taught Emanuele and I how to do bead weaving on a loom.

Chad actually hired me to do some bead work for him shortly after I had arrived. He had so many orders that he was backed up and overwhelmed. It was pretty cool doing that; I had become really good and fast at bead-weaving. He paid me well for it, too. Sweet Serendipity again.

The more time we spent together, I could tell he was starting to like me as more than a friend. I had made many new friends with local artists and jewelers through him, with whom I was also learning to make jewelry. One of them made a comment one night that Chad wanted to marry me. Yikes! He was a really sweet guy but I didn't feel that way for him, so I started pulling back and eventually just stopped working with him.

Fred, who for me was just a friend as well, also hit on me and was quite unpleasant to me when I wasn't matching his desire.

So Steffi and I hung out a lot more and became really good friends. We spent pretty much every day together. She introduced me to taking the water taxi to different places and markets. I really enjoyed being with her. It was simple and easy. She also introduced me to this great mobile Chai place at the end of Kao Sarn Road run by this Rasta Thai guy. He was so tiny and had Rasta hair that was so big. He was awesome. I believe his name was Jim. He was the nicest guy. He had an old ox car frame on the back of his truck where he put a stone cauldron heated with coals and made Chai tea every night with snacks. This is where the travelers would gather and have fun. He also played the most amazing music and we would dance in the streets. It was a blast! We went there pretty much every night.

After about a month I felt an urge go back to Seaview and retouch some of my experiences. I wanted to reclaim some parts of me that got fragmented when I was there last.

It felt so good to be travelling again! I decided to go by bus because it was cheaper, but was reminded why I the last time I had told myself I would never do the bus again! It was so uncomfortable and took way too long.

When I got to Surrathani, I encountered a very dangerous situation when I stepped off the bus. One that to this day when I consider what could have happened to me and almost did, I shudder.

As I mentioned, earlier travel agencies have a system for going from the mainland to the island where an affiliated travel agency will pick you up when you arrive to Surrathani to bring you to their agency until it's time to catch the ferry to the Island; at which point they will bring you to the ferry.

It had been a 12-hour bus ride, I had barely slept when we arrived. Having sat at the front of the bus, I got off first in my groggy state. As I stepped down there was this rather tall Thai man standing right in front of me. He asked to see my travel stub to identify if I was with his travel agency. This was the standard procedure I remembered from my last time in Thailand, so I didn't question him when he said for me to wait to the side, that I was to go with him.

I stood there for a few minutes and saw all the other passengers gathering to the opposite side of where he had told me to stand. It seemed odd to me that I might be the only one so I went up to him, getting closer to the bus and the group of people and tapped him on the shoulder.

When he turned around I showed him my ticket again and asked him if he was sure I was to go with him. He said, yes, yes, I was to go back to where he had originally told me to stand. I still felt a little uncertain but turned to go there anyway.

In the moment I started turning back I heard a loud woman's voice yelling *"Excuse me, you, you over there."* She repeated that sentence about three more times when I finally turned around and saw this tiny Thai woman literally jumping up from behind all the tall travelers, waving to me. I did the usually gesture of pointing to myself with a questioning look and she yelled *"Yes, you come here to me!"*

As this exchange with her was happening I hadn't noticed that the tall Thai man disappeared into the crowd as I had turned and went toward her.

When I reached her she grabbed my ticket and pointed to a group of passengers and said I belonged over there with them.

My whole body was instantly chilled to the core, and I am sure I must have turned the whitest shade of white at the realization of what had just almost happened. It was like the blood had drained out of me.

Who knows what that man had planned for me. I thank God that this small woman saw me and basically rescued me from what surely would have been a terrifying and horrible experience. Bless.

We got to the travel agency where I sat, drank some Thai iced tea that they offered and slowly processed the shock in my nervous system until it was time for them to take us to the ferry several hours later.

Being on the ferry, feeling the ocean, sun, and breeze, brought me back, I was so happy to be there and looking forward to returning to Seaview Rainbow.

To my surprise and great joy, Loreene was still there! My anchor! It was so great to see her again. I shared with her all my experiences since I last saw her, she shared some of her journey as well and we picked up where we left off. I had hoped my Puppy would be there but I found out from Loreene that Oi the owner had poisoned all the dogs about a month after I left. That broke my heart. I was friends with his wife Pan, but from that day on I ignored him completely.

Soon after my arrival I began doing Yoga with her again every day. She would make us lovely food for lunch afterwards just like before. It was so good to be back. She also had mango trees, guava trees, and papaya tree on her property that were ripe and ready to eat! Every day we had fresh fruit. Mmmmm. Heaven!

I stayed in the same bungalow Emanuele and I had been in., it was the closest to the water and the furthest from the meeting and eating area

The sign we made was actually still standing on the beach where we had installed it and it looked great. It hadn't weathered at all in the year.

I spent a lot of my time meditating, journaling and reflecting on everything that had happened when I was there with Emanuele. I could feel how it was a very important and wise choice for me to go back to Thailand to do this processing and integrating. I was so grateful to be there. The risk I was taking financially going there was well worth it.

Being back at Seaview really helped me deeply integrate, and it grounded me more. It wasn't just a trip, a dream/nightmare, which is what it had partly felt like when I was in Switzerland. It was real. It had happened.

In my time there aside from doing Yoga with Loreene I enjoyed the beach, collected shells, and swam a lot, both in the ocean and in my sweet water lake.

A traveler at Seaview told me that a full-moon party was going to be happening at Haadrin Beach again. I was excited about that and mentioned it to Loreene to see if she would join me. She said she would meet me there towards evening time.

When the day came I chose to walk there along the beaches. It took about 2.5 hours to get there. Walking is such good medicine, especially when it's such a beautiful walk. I soaked it all in and felt deeply lifted and nourished by all that Nature was offering me. Every movement of the waves soothed me, my nervous system was starting to unwind and relax again. What a relief!

I stopped along the way to get a fresh juice and something to snack on. It was so hot, I absolutely loved living in a sarong and light top and walking barefoot everywhere. My favorite thing ever. I felt so at home in Thailand. This time, it was the complete opposite of how I had felt almost exactly a year ago when I had arrived and was so afraid. Now look at me I thought. It's amazing how much we can grow and change in just one year or less.

I got to Haadrin and gathered memories and reflected some more. I walked up to the cabin I had stayed in at Serenity Bungalows, then had lunch in the same restaurant I used to eat at and watched some movies.

Later I went swimming in the beach that had taught me about letting go. My heart and soul felt happy and content for the first time in such a long time. What a nice thing to feel after what I had just gone through where I had feared never coming to such peace in myself again.

Loreene was going to be there soon, so I just hung out and visited some shops until she came, I was looking forward to having a night of fun and dancing.

The full-moon party is pretty amazing It happens on the beach where there are several bars set up along it playing different music so we can dance on the beach in the beautiful moonlight. It was great fun.

There was a call center in one of the shops so I called my father to say hi. I hardly had any contact with him and my family since the previous year. Though on one hand I could feel his joy talking to his daughter again, but as usual, in no time he was on me about wasting my life. I could feel myself shrinking and withdrawing deep into myself. Why do I even bother I asked myself at the end of the call.

Of course as a parent, he is concerned, but for me, who I was at that time, every time he said that it pushed me further away from him. He didn't see me and didn't try to either, at least that was how it felt. I had no real urge to go home. I felt very estranged, especially since I hardly had any memories of my life before 18. My memories were more like a movie preview with fragmented scenes that described the basic story. More recent memories had returned gradually, but I still didn't have full access to my history and I felt no emotional connection to them at all.

He asked me to come home for a visit for Christmas. I wasn't ready. I told him I would call him again in a few weeks.

When Loreene arrived and we were sitting grabbing a bite to eat, I spoke with her about this conflict and confusion in me around my family. That I didn't want to go but somehow felt obligated. She suggested I shouldn't go if it didn't feel right or wasn't the right time. I decided to go with that and agreed with her, though I still felt conflicted.

We ate a nice dinner together and then danced the night away in the water under the sparkling moonlight. I tried to dance the tension out of my body that had lingered after that conversation with my father. Dancing is another great medicine for healing that has helped me so much in my life.

The next morning we headed back to Seaview together by boat after having a yummy breakfast with lots of fruit.

When we got there, I saw this new guy had checked in who looked just like Emanuele from a distance: same hair, same kind of clothing, even the same posture and movement patterns. It was so unreal that I had to literally shake my head a bit to ward off weird feelings that were rising up my spine as if I was in the Twilight Zone!

We met later that day in the restaurant. His name was Dino. It was beyond words seeing him. He looked so much like Emanuele. Quite the orchestration of life, really. In the end it actually helped with my memory of events and to integrate them. Life is truly amazing!

There were no other major events to share there of any great consequence in my remaining time at Seaview. I relished every moment I was I was there.

As I was feeling more integrated and complete in my time on the island I decided to go back to Bangkok and try to find a job. I was running low on money again.

I caught the ferry from Tongsala then the train back to Bangkok as before and I went back to the Peachy Guest House to get a room. It felt like home. Steffi was still there too! Awesome! I was so happy for that.

We started looking for work together. A few days later we found a listing on a bulletin board looking for Native English Speakers to teach conversational English. We phoned and met the guy who had put up the posting. He had a job for each of us. He sent me to teach English at a plastic factory. I would be teaching the owner and her two managers. Steffi was sent somewhere else. *How cool was that, I thought.* I started right away the next day.

I took the bus for an hour to get there every day. I was getting into the rhythm of Bangkok. Before I would just stop over in Bangkok and wanted to get away as fast as possible, I didn't like it at all because it was stinky and noisy. Now, though, because I had friends and a life there, I didn't mind. I found I actually enjoyed it.

I showed up at the company and was directed to an office where first I met the owner. She then called in her managers and I started teaching them English. They were all so sweet and kind to me. It was a joy being there with them. Every day I came to work they had a plate of my favorite fruits waiting for me. Teaching them was a lot of fun.

A few weeks later when it was my birthday, they bought me gifts and even took me for dinner. They loved me and adopted me like family. It was so lovely.

I spoke to my dad again on my birthday. He asked me to come again, he said it had been too long, and that my Grandmother was getting old and wanted to see me, too. I said I didn't have the money to come, that I was working and maybe later down the road I would come. He offered to send me the money I needed to get a ticket so I could be there by Christmas. I really didn't want to go and was actually afraid I would lose the peace I had found. But, I realized it had to happen sooner or later, I needed to face whatever I had to face to heal completely, so I finally said okay, against every fiber of my being.

I wanted to have some time to keep working and anchoring myself before going so I got a ticket for almost 3 weeks later on the 26th of December. We would have a Christmas celebration later since I wouldn't arrive until one day after our usual traditional Christmas dinner at my Grandmothers.

I was so happy that I gave myself the next three weeks to prepare, I really getting nervous about this visit. It had been more than two years since I was there when I went to the World Healing Meditation. I was a completely different person in so many ways, and still healing from everything I had experienced those years away. My family had absolutely no idea what I had been going through. I knew they would meet me with their projections and ideas from the past, I questioned if I was strong enough to withstand that.

Even though I felt back in life again more myself compared to where and how I was months before, but there was still so much in my nervous system that was sorting itself out, unraveling and healing. As the days progressed I began to doubt my decision to go back to Toronto.

I continued teaching the next few weeks, then I returned to Seaview for one last visit with Loreene, to get her guidance on how to navigate this. She still said I shouldn't go if I feel the way I do; to wait until it really feels right, but I felt guilty somehow, that I had to. It was just a week away now.

I stayed there for four days, doing lots of Yoga, weaving, and meditation. My uneasiness kept growing. It felt like a daunting 100-foot wave was coming toward me and would swallow me if I wasn't careful. Deep breaths, I reminded myself every time I felt the presence of the wave.

No turning back now, I thought. I tried to rearrange my thinking to see the possible positive outcomes that could come from this, that it might actually be exactly the right thing for me to help me get more memories back.

I caught the night ferry and arrived to Surathani in the wee hours of the morning, it was still dark. I caught a tuktuk which is a bit similar to a rickshaw, from the ferry to the train station. I had no orientation as to where I was when I got stepped off the ferry it stopped at a different location then the day ferry. I had to trust that the driver would take me where I wanted to go. Driving through the hilly countryside in the dark, I had many moments of questioning, praying ang and hoping this guy was taking me to the train station, it was a long ride and I was so tired I had a hard time keeping my eyes closed. The stars were magnificent. So bright an beautiful.

I was six hours early for the train when I thankfully arrived at the station, so I decided to sleep on a park bench at the station for a few hours until the restaurants and shops started opening.

When I woke up I still had a few hours to go before my train so I went to a little store and bought some pastels and paper to draw while I waited. Steffi had inspired me by her pastel drawings so I decided to give it a try myself.

Then I went to a restaurant and had a bite to eat and drew until the train came. The time went by quickly and before I knew it, I was on the train.

I met a group of young Thai guys on the train, they were a lot of fun. One of them said he fell in love with me and gave me a bracelet of his to remember him by. It was so sweet and made the trip go by fast until they got off. The last part of my trip I made eye contact with this beautiful mature Thai woman. We shared our food; it was beautiful. I preferred traveling third class on the trains because I connected with the people so beautifully. The previous year I had done that once, too. It was a night train and was so full. I sat with three mature Thai men. We also shared our food; lots of smiles and took turns sleeping on newspaper on the ground between us. What an amazing adventure.

It was nice being back in Bangkok. I spent about another five days there, visiting with friends and taught two final English classes to the lovely women from the plastic company.

They took me out for a farewell dinner and actually cried that I was leaving; they wanted me to stay. It was so beautiful. I stayed at the owner's home that night and she set up the movie *Dances with Wolves* for me because at some point I had mentioned that I loved that movie. Such beautiful people. And, talk about completing a circle. I had come to Thailand to process and integrate everything that had happened with Ivan and now on my last night they played the movie with which I had connected with Ivan the most. Wow! The Universal Laws of Attraction and Resonance are truly amazing. We continually attract what and how we are and what we need based on the most constant and strongest frequencies we broadcast. Again and again I see confirmations of those Laws at work in our everyday lives. Most of us don't realize we are constantly creating our reality based on our beliefs and perceptions. That's the real magic in each of us and in life.

For my last night, Steffi and I went to the Chai place again and had a great time with all the friends we had made. Jim was sad to see me go, too, and wanted to see me the next day before my flight to say good-bye. It was a beautiful and joy filled last night in Bangkok. I was sad to go.

The next day when Jim and I met, he had brought me the most delicious Indian food that he had prepared for me to bring with me to eat on the plane. What a sweetheart. I couldn't wait to eat on the plane so I ate it in the waiting area. It smelled so good my mouth had been watering since he gave it me, so I opened and nibbled a bit until we were called to board the plane. Mmmmmm. It was so delicious! I still remember how my taste buds danced in glee with every bite.

Since I was planning to return to Thailand as soon as possible I left a full backpack of my belongings in the storage room at Peachy's Guest House. I said my good-byes and off I went to meet the 100-foot wave waiting for me back in Ontario.

My flight had an over-night stop-over in Japan, for which I was so grateful, it gave me more integration and preparation time. I went out for a short excursion in Japan the next morning before my flight. What an incredible place. I had remembered that a traveler I met said they taught English in Japan because they paid so well which enabled them to travel for several months without having to work. Being in Japan in that moment I considered doing that as a possibility when I returned to Thailand.

It was a smooth flight to Toronto, though the closer I got I could feel my body starting to shake. No turning back now! Here I go leaping into the unknown again!

8

RECONNECTING

Over the years of my life,
How many times have I looked at my face in the mirror?
How many different faces have I seen and projected?
How many different roles I have lived and played.
Life is truly a miracle.
Full of wonders and magic.
I have not yet come to understand,
Who I am,
Why I am,
The mysteries of life, my life, my soul.
Will I ever learn?
Will I ever know?
Will I ever understand?
All the different layers and aspects that make me, me?
I really want to.
What an adventure.
What an incredible journey of exploration and discovery.
- Journal Entry June, 1994, Germany, 23 years of age

The moment I disembarked the plane when we arrived in Toronto I was shaking so much inside that my hands and body were actually trembling. When I went through customs, the officer looked at me and said, "I see you are really nervous, how come?". I told him I was seeing my family for the first time in two years and was nervous. He obviously saw I was telling the truth, asking no further questions he let me through.

When I saw my dad in the crowd I felt the blood drain from my face and my whole body felt it was going pale. I felt no emotional connection at all; I knew he was my dad, but I felt totally disconnected. It was very disorienting and scary. I had been hoping I would feel something more. But I didn't. I felt nothing but numb inside.

Within me, I felt like a part of me wanted to panic and freak out, so I took very deep breathes to try to calm myself and did my best to pretend I was okay.

Clearly I was different from when he had last known me. I could see that he could see that. But still, I tried to keep up appearances. My father is a man of questions. Until I grew and healed in myself enough to see and know him as an individual with his own soul journey and experiences that made him who he is, his questioning always felt more like an interrogation and would trigger me emotionally very easily. Since I was always feeling-oriented and he was logic-oriented, it was hard for me to open to him. We were like polar opposites. As he asked me his questions, I struggled to be present and not be reactive.

The drive was awkward. The question was always, "What are you going to do with your life?" or, "You're wasting your life traveling," or, "You should go back to school." I know he meant well and only wanted the best for me according to his definition of life, but that way of questioning felt invasive and dominating to me. He had absolutely no idea who I was anymore nor what I had gone through, and I didn't feel I could share it with him, or anyone in my family.

That's what happens in many families, when we feel mis-perceived and dominated; that family members' perceptions about us are not accurate, which then limits our ability to express ourselves authentically as we are, because the space is clearly not there. We end up feeling there is no space to be who we are. The only thing we can do to self-preserve is to distance and armour ourselves, internally, and like me, externally as well.

If I had felt fully embraced in my expressions of me, and had the room to be and develop me, there would be no need to go so far away. I never felt that way though.

Our family was so fragmented and no one dealt with the trauma, it was all just pushed aside, building up under the surface. '*You just have to get over it and move on,*' was the motto.

Well, sorry, that doesn't work.

That's ultimately why I left home at 18, without consciously knowing that that was the underlying reason I left.

My soul or inner being somehow knew I could not grow into and become who I needed to be in that environment. It was a feeling that in order to grow I had to leave. It's just like in nature. We need the right and precise environment to flower and grow fully to what we can become.

The last time my father had seen me, I was dying my hair red, modeling, and wore fashionable clothing. Now, here I was, looking like a hippie, completely withdrawn, burning incense, singing mantras, and a vegetarian. I can only imagine what a shock it was for him! Now, I laugh at the thought of it! Poor guy! I was also nowhere near as joyful or expressive as I had been before. That part would have surely been painful for him to see.

When we got to the house it all felt so surreal. I felt strange seeing my sister, too. We chatted a bit, then I excused myself to go to my room, saying I was jet lagged. That was my excuse for not spending much time with them for the coming days until it was time to head to my Grandmothers for a few days to have our belated Christmas dinner. I don't have a lot of memories from being at my grandmothers except feeling perpetually overwhelmed and suffocated internally by what felt like judgmental and upset perceptions of me coming from everyone. I felt so out of place.

My dad has always had a genuine kindness to him. As a way to try to meet me he brought me to a used leather coat store in a neighboring town so he could buy me leather that I could work with doing my crafts. I remember his confusion about what happened to me, why I was so estranged and his worry. At the time though, it just irritated me and made me feel trapped. I can only imagine now how he felt. I was grateful for the leather and his effort.

I had met a man named Raphael from Germany in one of my walks along the beach in Thailand that said something that has never left me and has helped me innumerable times since then.

He said that no matter what we are going through, we need to stay active, keep moving forward. Whatever that is, walking, creating, writing, art, that the way through life's challenges is remaining active. Otherwise we stagnate. Doing the leather and beadwork was my way of staying engaged in life and keeping active.

Once we returned from my grandmothers I spent a lot of time in my bedroom, doing leather and beadwork, journaling, meditating, and crying. Niel and two of his friends had actually ordered leather pouches from me with beadwork. It was a good way for me to spend my time.

My mother had moved back to Canada a year after I moved to Europe and now lived just 15 minutes away from my fathers home. I was nervous about seeing her again.

I didn't mentioned earlier that she had come to see me in Locarno that summer when I was recovering from the mushroom trip. She came for a few days after having visited Rheinhold., I was in the depth of going through all my inner trials and confusions. It was intense, and often times her being there caused great disorientation in me. I felt such a deep disconnection with her as well, but had to try to keep up appearances while she was visiting of everything being "normal" to navigate my time with her there.

It was a multi-layered visit. She got upset with me again in the first days of being with me, as usual, because I wasn't how or what she thought I should be. We had a big blow-out, which given what I was going through, you can imagine how super hard it was to navigate. I managed by escaping into nature on my own those first days as often as I could.

As had always been the pattern, after her initial big explosions, things would smooth over. But still, I never shared what was happening in me, there wasn't the space to do so. I knew she would bombard me with all her judgements and interpretations, so I didn't bother.

Most of my memories from her visit are very vague which is why I didn't mention her visit earlier.

I brought her into Nature a lot in the coming days, which helped balance me because I always felt more grounded in Nature. Since I couldn't handle being alone in my apartment with her for too long Nature was the perfect medicine.

In her last days with me in Locarno, we did eventually share some fun and nice moments together. We jumped into the lake with all our clothes on one hot sunny day. For me that was something normal, but for her it was so outside her normal comfort zone.

She ended up enjoying it so much! It was like she became temporarily freed from her world of coping mechanisms control and safety so that her inner little girl could come out and play. It was really quite beautiful to experience her that way. It is still her most cherished memory. Mine too.

Now, here I was back in Pickering and I would see her again soon too, I was really nervous even though our last memories together were good ones. She was always so unpredictable, it was like walking on egg shells all the time.

When I did see her it was awkward but manageable. I experienced a lot of dissociation where she was concerned, but I got through. I only visited her a few times. Each time it was the same. Her criticizing me, putting down my father

140

etc., etc., which is why I didn't spend much time with her. It was exhausting how constantly negative she chose to be.

She was entangled in her pain and the distorted beliefs and perceptions that pain had created in her mind about life and others. Just like every one of us does until we delve deeper into our hidden shadows and patterns.

Even though I already understood a layer of that truth and insight, her negative and reactive patterns still triggered me, especially since nothing had been resolved since her disowning me before going to Thailand. The less time with her was better lest internal bombs got triggered again.

* * *

We have developed a beautiful and loving relationship now, it took many years to get to the point where that was possible though. Every time I had attempted to reconnect to her in the past, her abusive and manipulative patterns always came up again and again.

In the coming years she had "disowned" me fifteen times. The fifteenth time was when I decided to cut my connection with her completely so I could have time to do my own healing work relating to her.

I wanted to be able to reach the point that I could feel and see her original innocence, for she too was once an pure child full of joy, wanting to love and be loved. I wanted to heal myself to the point that I could fully understand her and with that understanding come to a place of genuine love and acceptance of all of her.

I had always believed I needed her to acknowledge her abuse in order to heal. Without consciously realizing it I had made my healing depend on her actions. If that's the case, the chances of my healing were pretty small. Coming to the realization it is my actions and choices that will bring me healing was a key insight. My healing depended on me, not anyone outside of me. I had to step out of being a victim.

As I gradually came to understand, more and more, that she was simply caught in her trauma and living by the coping patterns she had created to survive, my compassion for her grew and I realized her treatment of me wasn't personal against me.

Though of course it impacted me personally and a part of me wanted that to be recognized by her if we were to ever have a healthy and functional relationship again, I couldn't depend on that happening. Based on the past, I highly doubted that she would, so I made my peace with that as well.

When I did arrive to that inner place of love and acceptance, a miracle happened: she acknowledged her abuse and apologized. What magic! The world is our mirror in so many ways!

* * *

After about a week of being immersed in my family, I was feeling so stifled, I needed to get out of the house. I decided to call Andre. He had supported me that summer with letters of encouragement, and similar sharing of wisdom as Peter did, to help me understand what was happening in me. I felt he was someone who saw and understood me, and I needed to feel that.

Andre invited me to come for dinner with him and some friends. So I caught the train downtown and met them at the restaurant. I felt strange with him too though, which I didn't understand; he had always been someone I trusted. Something felt off, but I couldn't place it.

After dinner I was to stay at his place on the fold-out sofa in his living room since there were no more trains going back to Pickering.

I was sitting down on a chair in the living room after we arrived to his home when he started caressing my hair and touching my shoulder in a very sexual and intimate way.

I flinched and said, "Please don't do that, it wasn't invited." In that moment he stood up straight and yelled at me with the loudest thundering voice you can imagine, "You ungrateful bitch! It's because of me that you have the spiritual life you have, I signed my name for you in Heaven through the White Brotherhood!"

I was in shock. He kept yelling at me and told me if I dared leave the house he would curse me to darkness and then he left the room.

Shaking to my core, I made my bed and pulled out my journal that I always carried with me, and wrote the experience trying to process it. I went there looking for a friend, for comfort and care, and now I was being terrorized. It shattered me. So much so that I seriously couldn't discern, was I a bitch for denying him? Having my journal with me helped me to write out and sort all my conflicted thoughts and feelings. I was also really afraid of being cursed.

I ended up being trapped there, because of my fears, for three days. He didn't physically harm me but he was definitely not the same friend I had once known, he was mentally ill and feeding my head with all this dark and twisted stuff. I was afraid to leave because of his curse so I just sat there, pretty numbed out by the trauma of it all, and listened. It was terrifying.

I wrote in my journal every day, trying to figure out what to do. I couldn't get a break, one painful experience after the other knocked me down. Why was this happening to me? I was so confused. Am I self-righteous? Did I do something to offend God?

No, I finally affirmed to myself in my journal, that's impossible, God is love. I started strengthening that belief with affirmative self-talk the best I could. To gain the courage to leave.

I had experienced so much emotional volatility in my childhood that it would make me freeze. Which is what I did in this experience. I felt paralyzed to do anything. That is what happens when you have been traumatized, it's what many people don't understand. When you are caught in freeze mode of your nervous system you are temporarily cortically impaired to do anything until the freeze response thaws and your reasoning mind can kick in again.

On the third night he had a woman friend over. They had been drinking and finally went to bed. My reasoning mind was getting stronger so I took the opportunity at 4 in the morning to escape. I swear it felt like I had just left a vampire's lair.

I walked around downtown Toronto for a few hours, my body shaking, trying to walk it off. Then I grabbed a coffee and took the Go Train home and went to bed without a word to anyone. Talk about processing overload.

I stayed in bed for several days, I said I was sick and retreated more into myself. I had felt so good in Thailand. I really wished I had stayed. Why couldn't I remain in my joy of life there?

One day I thought of Gennie, from the World Healing Meditation. I still had her phone number in my address book so I called her. She lived on her own now.

We had been briefly in contact that summer when I was trying to reconnect the dots of my life. She was happy to hear from me and invited me to come stay with her if I wanted. Gratefully, I went to her place.

It was nice to see her again. In our sharings of our life she told me of a dance practice she was learning called Martial Dance. It incorporated Contact Improv with, Tai Chi and Aikido and Feldenkreis techniques. It sounded fascinating to me and with my having explored movement meditations with Loreene, I was keenly interested. I asked if I could go to the dance class with her sometime. She said I would need to talk to the teacher first. She told him about me, then we had a conversation on the phone. He asked why I was interested. I told him how I loved dancing and what I had been learning in Thailand. He said that sounded great, to come with Gennie to the next class.

I went to the dance class and absolutely loved it! It felt like ecstasy to me I remember being so nervous in the change room and looking at myself in the mirror and mumbling, "you can do this" before heading into the dance studio. It's always a bit frightening stepping into the unknown. At the end of the class I was a glowing tomato! So much energy and joy flowing through me.

I continued to go to the classes every chance I got for the time I was there. It took me deep into my body, and expanded my understanding and awareness profoundly. It was deep and beautiful. In one of the classes I was sharing a generalization of how "people feel." About something I don't even remember now. My teacher looked at me deeply then redirected my awareness to see that I was using the generalization to cover the fact that I was actually feeling that way. He told me to use an "I" statement when I express those thoughts. That confused me and I started to shake inside. When I replaced the "they" with "I," I burst into tears. These are the ways we keep our true inner world hidden in plain sight. We don't speak directly about ourselves, it's always projected outward instead of inward. That rocked my world and shifted me in a whole new direction of self-discovery. I was hooked!

I also met a nice man, named Neil in my time in Toronto who owned a Healing Centre at Bloor and Christie in Toronto. I had phoned inquiring about his floatation sensory deprivation tanks. We hit it off so great on the phone. I made an appointment for the next day. We became really good friends and spent a lot of time together. He was so kind and loving, exactly what I needed. We shared some intimacies, cuddled and kissed, which was the most I had felt comfortable doing since this journey after Thailand. I could see I was slowly healing.

I shared with him what happened with Andre. He knew a little about him and said he wasn't surprised. A few days later he introduced me to a friend of his who helped lift the dark energy remaining around me from that experience and lifted the curse. I really felt it leave. I also had to do a special bath for a few days to help restore my energy and rebuild my aura from the blast it experienced. Well, I sure felt better after that.

Neil did some other healing on me too, called Radionics It's a form of frequency healing. I could feel the shifts right away. Again, such a blessing. Yes, there were more hard knocks, but grace-filled blessings and helpers always showed up along the way to help me. Always the right people and situations fell into alignment just when I needed them most.

That is a key message in my experiences. When we connect at a deeper level to our-self and life, and we are wholly committed to healing and changing, there is an energy, a supportive life-force that comes to our aid. It is that way for everyone. Call it Providence, call it God, call it what you will, it is a real force of Good that governs this universe that is always available to us when we seek and are open to grow. Our openness and commitment is the catalytic force that activates this flow of support. Staying in a place of victimhood does not activate the magic. We have to open and extend ourselves to Life. We have to give it our all, to gain it all. We need to reach out to higher octaves of wisdom, knowledge and learning in every moment. When we do, Life/God meets us there.

One night, Neil took me to an Aboriginal event. There was a guy playing the flute there about whom I had read an article in one of Andre's papers the year before. He had been on the streets for many years, addicted to virtually every drug, then one night he had a dream of an orca whale crying. It penetrated his nervous system and shook him up so deeply. He took it as a message to go back to his elders and heal. Which he did. One of the medicines the elders gave him was a flute he was supposed to teach himself through his prayers. I had been deeply touched by his story when I read it back then, and was really looking forward to hearing him play.

The first note from the flute leaped into my heart and cracked it wide open. I cried. It was so beautiful. I later met him briefly at the end of the event and thanked him, expressing how much it moved and touched my heart hearing him play.

Afterwards, when we got back to Neil's, I knew he had a flute in his closet, so I asked if I could try, inspired by what I had heard. He said of course. It was a golden side-playing flute, a little harder to play then a front-playing flute. I tried and tried until I got a note. My heart sprang for joy when I finally did. I knew in that moment, with every fiber of my being that I had to play the flute.

The next morning, I went to a store called Inti crafts -- a serendipitous name, I thought since the Peruvian Shamans name was Inti. I bought myself a $5 bamboo flute from Bolivia and started to play. Knowing that this guy was self-taught somehow gave me permission to try it myself.

In my remaining time I also saw Iona a few times while I was in Toronto She was busy a lot of the time I was in her store. It was nice just being there again and near her when I could be even though we didn't have much personal time together. She always saw my light and soul, always lifting me up and encouraging me. She even said she admired me for my efforts and dedication to grow and heal. That felt like superfood for my heart, being seen like that.

I bought many new crystals and a beautiful Beaver Medicine Shield. Beaver medicine in Native teachings has to do with building one's life, among other things. When I saw it I just loved it. When Iona told me the teachings that go with it, I knew I had to get it.

In the end. I was hardly at home during my visit once I had started going downtown and only saw my mother a few short times.

Soon it was already time to leave. I had bought a return ticket from Toronto to Zurich, since it was cheaper than a one-way. I had no intentions of returning to Toronto anytime soon though.

My apartment was waiting for me. I was feeling stronger again through my experiences dancing and the special time I had with Neil. He and his healing modalities played a huge role in my moving forward for which I am always grateful. I looked forward to going back and integrating everything and I felt confident I would find another job, then go back to Thailand as soon as possible. That was my plan.

You know that joke? How do you make God laugh?

You tell Him your plans.

Well, I never could have imagined what was in store for me.

Here comes another wave! And it's a dozy!

9

TIME TO LET GO

Always be aware and know that God/Spirit is with me,
Guiding me each step of the way,
Even if I sometimes don't realize it.
There is a purpose for every happening.
Have faith in that and in the experiences that are given to me,
Especially the hard and painful ones that seem to be too much to
bear or too overwhelming.

Within those moments are the greatest teachings,
if I can overcome my ego and emotions to open my eyes
to see clearly what is actually happening.
Keep the faith and allow myself to be guided to what is truly right.

I have had enough experiences to know that this is how it works.
Be patient and trust.
The tools I need will be made available to me
in the right times and right way when needed.
I am never alone.
Ho!
- Journal Enrty June 10, 1993, 22 years old

After arriving back to Switzerland I took the train and finally got home to my apartment in Locarno. It was nice to be in my space again. I didn't have much money so I had to get on it to find a new job. I found one in Ascona at a restaurant. I put in my application for the work visa and waited.

In the meantime, while I was waiting to get my work visa, I found out that Inti was in Brienze Switzerland again, where I had been the last time. He was offering another healing workshop. I felt the inner pull to go there and was luckily sponsored in by the Schweibenalp Meditation Center where the workshop was, so I didn't have to pay.

Being there helped me a lot and I made a new friend named Heiri. He had been studying with Inti and other Shamans for many years and practiced Shamanism himself. I did another sweat lodge and we did drumming and singing like the first time. It helped me integrate.

Inti gave us all a healing stone. I had a bunch of leather with me for making my crafts so I made a bunch of mini medicine bags for everyone to put their stone in. Doing my crafts always grounded me. It was fun. It brought me great joy making them. At break time I quietly placed them on Inti's altar so he could pass them around. Everyone loved them.

I was there for just a few days then went back to Locarno to hopefully get the news my visa was there, and cross the border over to Germany to go get it.

It wasn't ready yet. It was taking a lot longer to receive the work visa than usual. While waiting I did a few trial shifts at the restaurant and got paid for it, so that helped me financially., I still felt fragmented though, which challenged me a lot. Nonetheless I was still doing my work well I thought. I was always a hard and dedicated worker, that wasn't the issue, it was the part about interacting and relating with colleagues that was difficult because of my sensitivity. I was still learning how to navigate with my senses being so heightened.

One day my old bosses came in from the Discoteque. They knew my new boss. I guess everybody knows everybody in a small place like Ascona. I felt a bit awkward because I know they had a different interpretation of what happened to me, why I changed. They thought Ivan ruined me. From the outside, it could look that way, and there was some truth to it too, but he had also been a key in the beginning, freeing me to be me. I had dropped all my makeup; fancy clothes and things that weren't really me anymore. For that I will always be grateful to Ivan. But to them I had fallen.

They were politely friendly, but I could feel contradictory currents underlying the surface. I was concerned they might say something to my new boss that would make him change his mind about hiring me. The papers were already in process so I hoped it would come through soon.

A few days later I decided to phone the foreigner police to find out what was taking so long, if they maybe needed something more. They asked me where I was; I said I was there in Locarno in my apartment as a tourist. They told me to come down and see them the following Monday. I said sure.

Having no idea what was awaiting me, I went in Monday morning and showed them my passport, telling them I had called on Friday.

The man aggressively snatched my passport out of my hand and said to me "You have 24 hours to leave the country. There is a law that says you are to wait in an outside country for the answer to your visa, since you have been here this long you should know that!"

What just happened?

I was stunned and shaking. How did it happen? I expressed to him that I obviously didn't know that law, otherwise I wouldn't have called them. I expressed that I have been legal every year, paying my taxes, and no one had ever told me that I had to wait in a foreign country for the answer. Even the agency that filled out my application for me didn't tell me that when I told them I would remain in Locarno as a tourist. I always knew I had to pick up my visa in a foreign country, as I had done the years before, but I didn't know I had to wait there as well.

I told the officer that if I had known that, I would have gone to my stepfathers house in Germany. The officer didn't care, he scolded and patronized me. He filled out a long form, and asked me many questions. He wanted me to pay a fine. I said I had no money and that he would have to put me in jail. He let the fine go and gave me a sheet of paper I had to give up when I crossed the border within 24 hours.

Total shock set in. I couldn't stop my body from trembling.

I left there absolutely devastated and went to Brigitte's. There was nothing I could do. She suggested going to the main police department in Bellinzona. So I did, but they wouldn't give me the time of day. It was so odd, no one would talk with me. So I had to go and pack as much as I could.

A new friend that I had met in Brigitte's store, Gerd, offered to pay my rent so I wouldn't lose my things. We had only known each other a couple of weeks, so that was an incredible gesture. He was very kind. Brigitte and other friends put money together for me so I could leave. Again, another hard knock, but look at the grace and blessings that came to my aide.

Gerd brought me to the train station as well. I had phoned my stepfather earlier asking him if he would take me in. He said yes, of course! He was such a beautiful soul. Even though my mom had left him, he still treated and accepted me as his daughter. So off I went again with my drum, crystals, my flute, books, and a few clothes.

Rheinhold picked me up at the train station and took me to his home where I had spent almost every summer in my youth until I moved to Germany. I had a really good relationship with him, he was easy to get along with, and never forced any opinions on me, I was able to just be. He was a caring and generous man.

The first days there I just rested and sat in the garden, either writing in my journal or weaving.

One morning when I was reading a local paper and saw an ad from the same hotel where I had done my practicum for restaurant and hotel management. They were looking for a masseuse.

I didn't have official training, but I used to give Neil massages in exchange for the treatments I had with him and he told me many times to never get training, that I will lose my natural touch.

I had been unofficially taught by Peter, when he worked on me which Niel also knew. So I decided to phoned Neil and asked him if he would be willing to write a letter of recommendation for me. He's a Doctor of Chiropractic, so I thought that might have some influence. He said of course and faxed it to the employee hiring manager, Frau Bauer.

Frau Bauer had also been there when I worked at the hotel before. She accepted his recommendation and said okay. I was hired, but only temporarily until someone with papers came. I worked there for several weeks. It was weird at first being back in the Hotel, but I loved what I was doing, so it was good for me.

I drove Rheinhold's little moped every day to work through the Black Forest; it was beautiful. I was kept really busy and received great feedback and recognition of my abilities. That built me up a bit. It also was perfect being both at Rheinhold's and the Hotel because both marked the beginning of my journey in Europe, the beginning of me having the freedom to self-authoring my life. It helped me integrate and fill in many memory gaps.

"In every difficulty lies opportunity." Thank you, Albert Einstein, for helping me see and use all experiences as an opportunity to grow and learn.

A few weeks later I was able to go back to Switzerland to get my belongings. Heiri, my new Shaman friend, came and picked me up at Rhienhold's to bring me to Switzerland.

Gerd was still in Locarno, too, so they both helped me clear everything out and clean the apartment. My landlady was livid and accused me of lying that I wasn't thrown out. She was horrible. I didn't need that extra stress. I never would have left Locarno of my own accord. Ever! I was still hopelessly attached to Emanuele and I loved it there more than anywhere in Europe. I was devastated, but moving forward nonetheless.

While I was there I went to see Emanuele at the poll where he still worked and told him what happened. He was indifferent, still shut down. I said good-bye to him and all my friends. I dropped in to see Brigitte one last time and then headed back to the Black Forest. It was time to let go.

We stopped at Heiri's home on the way, where he gifted me a flute, now I had two flutes. He was also very kind. Apparently he told me that when he and Inti were standing together on the hill and I waved at them from the swing below, Inti had said to him "There's a real lady, who is in a really troubling time." Boy, was that true.

It touched me when he shared that. A part of me felt seen and valued. Good medicine that I needed.

When I got back to Bonndorf and went to the hotel, they told me they had found a new masseuse with papers. So that job was done. Now what? I still had my return ticket to Toronto that was coming up soon, but I really didn't want to go back. I had my new friends in Toronto, but I didn't feel comfortable going back to my Dad's, which is what I would have to do if I went back. I felt it would be too confining for my soul. My Dad is a kind and beautiful man, but we were just too different. Polar opposites, really. I was the free-spirited gypsy and he was the logical and rational one. I am the risk taker whereas he covets safety and comfort. Nothing wrong with that but that difference created a lot of clashing.

We have a beautiful relationship now, which I know couldn't have happened if I had gone back at that time. I had to heal first so I could create the space to let him be him and then get to know his heart rather than the dysfunctional patterning that had formed between us.

The day of the flight back to Toronto came and went. I remember sitting at Rheinhold's office desk the night before staring at the ticket and weighing the possibilities. In the end I let it go and had no idea what I was going to do next.

I just felt and knew going back to Toronto was not an option. I phoned the Swiss consulate to find out if there was any way to undo what happened because it was such an obvious mistake on my part. The man I spoke to said the file hadn't yet gotten to the head office, that he would look for it and get back to me. I found that odd that he didn't have any information yet, there was nothing more I could do but wait.

A few days later I received a call from Inti. Heiri told him what happened to me. He said he was going to come see me the next day if I was available that he would help me. I said sure, yes thank you.

That felt really nice that he was going to do that. When he arrived he said he wanted to take me to Frankfurt that he had a friend there where he has some things in storage. So we drove about 5 hours to get there. When we arrived we went to the home of his friend. She and Inti took me upstairs to where there was a storage room. He opened it and pulled out a large light turquoise backpack.

He unzipped the backpack and showed me all the jewelry, stone masks, and crystals that were inside, at least $10,000 worth for sure. He closed it back up and handed me the backpack. He said live off of this as much as you can, and whenever we meet again you can give me what is left over and half the profit.

Wow! So kind, so generous. I thanked him in awe that this was happening. What a gift of support. She invited us to stay the night; she was really nice and made us a nice dinner. We headed back early the next day.

He dropped me off and went back to Switzerland. I went to a neighboring town called Freiburg to see when they had markets so I could sell the jewelry. I had my jewelry-selling case already that I had made in Ascona, so on market day I went and got a stand. I did that three times, when I got a call from my cousin Alex to come stay with him in Berlin if I wanted. I said great, I would love to! I phoned a driving agency that orchestrates drivers and passengers throughout Europe, the Mitfahr Zentrale. I phoned for a seat in someone's car to Berlin. There was one spot available in two days' time.

Perfect. I got my things together, put some stuff in the attic and waited.

Rheinhold kindly brought me to Freiburg, where I would be meeting the driver at the train station. We would be driving through the night, arriving in Berlin in the wee hours of the morning.

The only drawback of this driving service is you never know who you will drive with. It was just me and him. He smoked the entire time and was playing heavy metal non-stop. Not so much fun. I didn't get any sleep at all, but I was grateful for the ride. With the train it would have cost me several hundred DMarks (the Gernman Currency at the time) this way it was only 60 DM. It's a great way to get around Europe for less than half the price of train or air fare.

Off I went with my drum, my flute, a few clothes, lots of crystals, books, a little bit of money and the backpack Inti had given me. The adventure continues.

10

ONWARD AND UPWARD

I feel alone,
Yet, the lives of millions carries on around me.
I am confused,
Yet, I can feel the wind through my fingertips.
I feel sad,
Yet the birds outside are still singing their beautiful songs.
I feel hurt,
Yet, the murmuring rivers journeying to the sea are still flowing.
I feel these things,
Yet, I am still breathing.
YES!
I am ALIVE!
The sun shines above me, nourishing me and whispering,
Grow!
What a wonderful world!
I am not alone!
I give Thanks!
-Journal Entry Sept. 26, 1994, Berlin, 23 years old

We arrived to Berlin at about 5:30 in the morning. The driver dropped me off somewhere on a side road. I had no idea where I was, the sun was just starting to rise giving a bit of light to the sleeping city.

I started looking for a phone booth to call Alex but couldn't find one anywhere. I walked around a lot looking and was beginning to feel some fear arise in me about not being able to be able to reach him. *There's got to be a phone somewhere,* I thought reassuring myself.

A one point in my search I saw an elderly lady walking her dog, the only person out on the street. I asked her where the nearest phonebooth was. She said there were no phone booths nearby but if I wanted to wait I could go up with her to her apartment and use her phone. How kind.

I gratefully waited, and then we went up to her apartment. We chatted a bit and she even offered to make me breakfast. So nice. I finally reached Alex and gave him the address where I was. He said he would be there to get me in about an hour. So I was fed and shared lovely company in the comfort of a cozy home while waiting for him. What a sweet way to begin my time in Berlin, with the kindness of strangers.

Alex came and got me and took me to his home, which was a shared co-op, similar in concept to Gennie's when I met her, and showed me the room I could stay in.

He lived with three other roommates. It was a sweet place with a nice green backyard where I spent a lot of my time. It became my little patch of Nature and refuge in the big city.

That last few days I kept hearing this melody in my head that somehow comforted me but I couldn't remember where I had heard it or what it was. One of his female roommates was a musician, so I hummed it for her and asked if she knew it. She said it was the song *Amazing Grace*. I then asked her if she knew the words. Turns out she did and she handed me a music book with the words in it. That song became my healing mantra. The melody made my heart feel good, and I learned the words, too. Beautiful song. I sang it to myself constantly.

Alex gave me an old bike I could use to explore and get around. On first day I rode all over the city and then came to a main tourist road called Kurfurstendamm Strasse.

I saw a young woman selling watches and jewelry. I decided to approach her and we started talking. I went to the restaurant in front of us and bought us a coffee. As we got to know each other and it was clear we clicked, I asked her if I could join her on her stand at all the markets she does. She smiled and said, ya, that sounds like fun. Her name was Andrea. My first day and look at the magic already.

The next day Alex took me to where he worked, which wasn't far from where I had met Andrea. I hung out with him there most of the day, and walked around a bit to get acquainted with the area. There was this beautiful large tree in the park that drew me. I went and sat by it, closed my eyes and meditated.

I really missed my tree in Locarno. The bizarre thing was that when I went back to Locarno when I had returned from my last trip to Thailand when I went to see my tree, it was gone. Out of all the trees in that little forest, mine, the one that I went to everyday for solace and grounding, had been chopped down. The only tree cut down in the whole park. It didn't make sense. What are the odds? Upon later reflections, that was already a big sign of life telling me it was time to let go.

I felt comfort sitting at this new tree, so I pulled out my flute and played a little. When Alex finished work he took me to dinner at an Indian restaurant that was close by. It was so yummy, I ended up eating there a lot.

I started selling the jewelry with Andrea at different markets, it was fun, and everyone really liked the jewelry I had. I was getting to know so many new people everywhere, making new friends at the markets. I was immersed in another whole new culture and experience. It was a good distraction from processing the traumas that had happened. I loved it. I also met a nice guy who sold incense, his name was Roland. He had spent many years learning the Tabla drum in India. He also let me sell with him at some other stands he had where Andrea didn't. We quickly became good friends. He also brought me to some amazing Indian restaurants. I was in heaven with such culinary delights.

After about a month I was starting to not feel comfortable at Alex's, he was becoming very sarcastic with me and it didn't feel good. He became very passive-aggressive making diminishing comments about me and my spirituality. Being in the same home with him was becoming unbearable.

When I shared my discomfort with Roland one day at the market, he said he had an extra space in his home if I needed somewhere to stay. He lived with one other roommate, and offered me to move in. A few days later I did. I was happy to leave Alex's. He was becoming too mean to me. I didn't need that energy coming my way.

I ended up finding part time work at two Indian restaurants. At one of them there was this kind man from Pakistan. He was quiet and gentle, I think in his late 30's. His name was Bhati. When he heard how I ended up in Berlin, he took it upon himself to help me get established.

For two months he bought me a bus pass and he bought me groceries every week to help me. No strings attached. He was very respectful and never crossed any boundaries.

He often took me out for dinner at other Indian restaurants, too. More blessings. If not for the kindness of strangers I wouldn't have made it very far. It lifted my heart and made me start trusting people again. I felt really taken care of and supported by life. I was so grateful for this new beginning.

One day at different market I mentioned to a new friend, who sold clothes, Claudia, about a kind of clove cigarette I had tried when I was with Emanuele. They tasted sweet and gave me a soft buzz. I used to smoke them sometimes after work that summer in Locarno when I was healing. A few puffs always took the edge off my stressed nervous system.

I asked if she knew where I might find them. She told me to look for an Indonesian restaurant since that's where they come from. They may sell them or at least know where to get them. Great idea!

I remembered then when I went for my interview to work at the Indian restaurant, I had passed an Indonesian restaurant. What serendipity! A few days later I went to check it out.

There was a young charismatic man that greeted me when I entered. His name was Yuri. He said he knew where to get the cigarettes, that he will get me some and I should come back in a week. We chatted for a few moments, he was curious where I was from, what I do. Then I left.

I went back the following week but he didn't have them, apparently the store he got them at was sold out. He offered me a juice and a bite to eat. He was seriously flirting with me. He had just opened the restaurant two months prior, with a woman friend he said he was married to for papers, but they were never a couple. They were going separate ways, apparently.

He said he might need help if I was interested in working there. With all my experience I definitely could contribute a lot. Something didn't sit right for me, though. I just said to him casually, *who knows, maybe*.

He wanted to meet again so he invited me to dinner later that week. I said sure, he seemed like a nice enough guy, but there was something I couldn't put my finger on. It wasn't huge, so I let it go. I assumed it was just me with my insecurities and traumas making me overly sensitive.

He mentioned about the possibility of my working at his restaurant again. I was happy where I was, I said.

The next day he brought me flowers at the Indian restaurant, that I worked at. He kept coming by to take me out or drive me home. I was living with a different friend by that time, Thomas, who lived closer to the restaurants I worked at and he had offered me his extra room. Roland's place was almost two hours away so it didn't work out for me to stay there. I got to know Thomas and his girlfriend well. They were really nice people, they really liked me too.

Yuri kept courting me, and I was starting to yield. There were a few times he made "off" comments when he dropped me off at Thomas's but I ignored it when I should have really paid attention.

I met his partner; she seemed nice, she was much older than him, about 25 years his senior. He told her he wanted me to run the restaurant and work with him. She seemed fine with it, since she had already stepped out of the business, but I had the feeling Yuri wasn't telling me the truth about the nature of his relationship with her. I kept prying, trying to find out if they were indeed lovers, which would change everything if that was the case, I would not go for that. He repeatedly assured me they were just friends. He said it was all good.

Subconsciously I think a part of me was looking for a place to land, so I convinced myself I was in love with him. I had genuine feelings of attraction for sure, but I amplified them beyond what they truly were out of my need to feel loved, safe and needed.

I finally said okay to his working proposition. They got me a work permit, which made me feel safe, because until that point I was always afraid of being caught without papers. Yuri had moved out of the home where he had lived with her. We had no apartment of our own, yet, so we lived in the restaurant the first month, sleeping behind the bar at night. Eventually we were able to stay at a friend of theirs who lived upstairs from the restaurant for a month, then I found us an apartment.

All of her friends treated me strangely, though. Not kind at all, they were very dismissive of me. Yuri said to not worry about it, that's just how they were, but I was getting suspicious, something didn't add up. If they had been only friends for papers, why would all her friends be so rude and disrespectful to me? I would have thought they would be happy he met someone with my experience and good heart.

Yuri was also slowly becoming very controlling, making the few friends I had made before meeting him feel very uncomfortable when they came in the restaurant -- until they just didn't come any more. When I would tell him that I wanted to go for a coffee with my friends he created a big conflict, he was becoming possessive and was emotionally manipulating me. I didn't need anybody else he said, I have him now and I have to take care of the restaurant and him.

I was still so fragile, trying to find my ground that had been ripped from underneath me. I was trying so hard to be and look strong in the world. I could feel myself becoming uncertain about my choices. I was starting to fear I was making a mistake being with him. But I stayed anyway.

He told me I was imagining things when I confronted him about there having been something more between him and his former partner. He very successfully caused me to doubt myself, undermining my confidence.

I was only 22, just turning 23 in December. Still so naive to so much, and still so broken underneath it all. To survive that brokenness I became somewhat numb.

I was pretty smart otherwise, but somehow he got into the subconscious beliefs I had that I was stupid, un-loveable, and that there was something wrong with me. He played that card regularly to put me in my place by telling me I was not loveable -- that it's no wonder Emanuele left me and why I hadn't found anyone to love me. Such cruel comments meant to undermine me. It's like I was in a kind of trance, from which I couldn't awaken. My nervous system was so shot already and now he was playing into my deepest traumas and fears. As we moved forward in time, he became more and more abusive.

I ended up finding out that he had indeed lied to me about the nature of his relationship with his former partner. They had been intimate until shortly before I came on the scene. When I found out from her directly, I told her what he had told me, but she refused to believe it. He had her and her friends so wrapped around his little charismatic fingers and convinced them he was someone he wasn't, as he had convinced me in the beginning. He was a hustler. for sure. Hustling her and all her friends who happened to all be very wealthy!

I found purpose in doing the restaurant work. It fulfilled me and gave me a structured activity that grounded me in spite of everything else.

The restaurant was a huge success, the two of us built it to what it became, that brought me joy and fulfillment. We were rated one of the top 10 restaurants in all of Berlin in 1995.

I put all my love and effort into every detail. I had made handmade menus from bamboo and leather with calligraphy, I burned incense and aromatherapy and played meditative music. Because the restaurant became my baby, too, I was reluctant to leave it so I just tolerated the situation with him. I also kept hoping that the man he was originally when we met would resurface. He never did.

Yuri also had a gambling problem. I had to practically beg to buy things for myself, while he would go gamble away the money I should have been earning. He was convinced he was going to win big. An addicts delusion.

A point came where I didn't recognize myself anymore. I became so skinny, and the only joy I had in the day was with the guests. That was enough for a while, but then it wasn't anymore.

After a year of sinking deeper and deeper I started asking, what happened to me? How did I lose touch so profoundly with everything that had lifted my heart and soul in joy previously? I had suppressed my spirituality with Yuri because he didn't believe in that stuff and I suppressed my heart in so many ways. Why would I even endure that? What hook did he have in me? I even had to hide my altar underneath the bed. Where did I go and how did he get so much control over me? These are the questions I started asking myself.

I decided something had to change. All my poems and journal writings were a protest now, to how I was being treated and how I had a right to be me. Like I was fighting for my life in my writings. It went way deeper than what the current situation was. I finally saw that. It went way back into my childhood and family story. That was a helpful insight. Then I remembered all my belongings were still at Rheinhold's home in his attic. I realized I needed go get them. Now!

I felt that by reclaiming my belongings there would be reflections of the me I felt I had lost touch with, the me that I was before all these traumas happened.

I arranged to go back to Rheinhold's using that driver service again. Yuri protested. I didn't care anymore; I just went. It literally felt like life or death in me. I had to go.

The guy that drove me was really nice; Christian was his name. He told me about a healer in Berlin that a friend of his had learned energy healing with. We had nice eight-hour drive, good music and good conversation. When we got to Rheinhold's we went upstairs to where his mom and dad had moved in recently. His mom made us a nice lunch, then Christian went on his way. He was going to be able to drive me back to Berlin too, at the end of the week, which was great!

I spent the coming days in the attic, sorting through my things, looking at pictures, reading my old journals. I was slowly coming out of the trance I had been in and back to myself.

I remembered Yuri often spoke about how much black magic there was in Indonesia. The longer I was at Rheinhold's it truly felt like coming out from under a spell. I seriously wondered if he hadn't maybe done something to me, or gotten somebody to. Maybe that is why he didn't like spirituality, just magic.

Whatever it was, I was waking up. With all his friends and his former partner he was so nice and charming, they had no idea how he was with me. I am certain if I were to have told them, they wouldn't believe me. He had them totally mesmerized.

Even with seeing through all that though, a part of me hoped I was wrong. That if I came back to myself, maybe he would be different with me.

It's illogical, I know, but I had those thoughts. Many people do who are in abusive relationships, that's why we stay, hoping they will finally see us and change. I sense a part of it for me was also not wanting to feel like a failure with another "broken relationship," so I hung on to the few morsels of good that I at one point saw and experienced in and with him. Like a wilted plant, I waited and hoped that I would be "watered" and cared for again. The fact is though, that unless the other person is actively engaged in becoming self-aware and wanting to grow together, the relationship will never work. I didn't know that then, though.

I decided that when I got back I was going to start doing the things I loved to do: dance, meditation, spiritual stuff -- and see what happens. I would no longer let him convince me to do otherwise.

Before I returned to Berlin, Heiri came to visit me. We went for a nice walk up my little mountain behind Rheinhold's home. I didn't fully disclose everything I was going through; I just wanted to deal with it on my own, and not involve any-one. He could see I wasn't happy though, and reminded me that I deserved to be happy. It was wonderful to see him, both because of who he is and also for the link he was in my life that connected me to everything good, vital and important to me.

Christian picked me up in the early evening when it was time to go back. My grandmother fed us again and gave us yummy baked goods for the road. She was an amazing baker! I slept most of the ride back. This time.

Christian dropped me off at the apartment. Yuri had been friendlier to me on the phone the few times we had talked. Maybe he realized he couldn't treat me badly anymore, I wished. He was nice when I arrived; even affectionate. What a surprise.

The next day, however, when I told him my plans to go to dance classes and go out with friends more often, he was not happy. "*Why do you need that for,*" he protested. "*Because I do,*" I replied And that was that. He didn't know how to respond, so he gave me the silent treatment. That was just fine with me. I was starting to catch on and not let him control me as much as I used to.

It was nice being back in the restaurant though. I loved it, it was my baby. Yes, they had opened it two months before I met him, but everything it became I knew because of me and the love and attention I gave it. He was a master chef, for sure that had its part in the success, but without the work I did at the front, my service and all the beautiful details I put in to the place, it wouldn't be half of what it became. I felt proud of that. I worked really hard to get it where it was. I put all my heart and soul into it. That's what made it possible to be in that situation for so long.

But was it worth it? I asked myself. *Was the relationship still salvageable? Should I stay?* These are questions I had asked myself more intently; I couldn't coast in the trance I was in anymore. I needed to go deep to uncover the answers.

I kept my word to myself and went dancing. I remembered that when I had first arrived to Berlin, before meeting Yuri, I would go to this Osho dance club all the time, almost every night really, they had the best music. They were open until 5 in the morning. In that time, I had gotten to know some of the Sanyasins that ran and worked at the place, and we had become friends. I hadn't realized how much I missed dancing, having been caught in the numbness that had taken over my life until then. I decided I was going to start going there more often too.

I discovered a dance practice called *Biodanza,* Translated it means *The Dance of Life.* Biodanza is a form of expressional dance exploring the essential aspects in our life that create who we are. It's a system of self-development that uses music, movement, and positive feelings to deepen self-awareness. The focus is to promote the ability to make a holistic link to oneself and one's emotions and express them. The music was phenomenal! There were high-percussion trance dances that were so liberating to me and connected me to me in new and deep ways. I loved it!

I also explored *The Five Rhythms* by Gabrielle Roth. It has a similar focus as Biodanza, personal transformation through movement and music, but uses a different framework, exploring the various rhythms of Nature, which is our Nature: Lyrical, Staccato, Chaos, Flowing, and Stillness. It was also a very releasing technique and the music that Gabriel Roth created for the classes was out of this world! Pure ecstasy!

After my first Biodanza class I went back to the restaurant where Yuri was preparing for the next day. He didn't say a word to me. He didn't even look up. I waited a few moments then asked him if he wasn't going to ask me how it was. His response? *"What do I get out of it? I don't care how it was!."*

Wow! I saw it all right there. He had no idea who I was, at all. He just wanted to mold the wounded puppy he had found to be what he wanted me to be. Clearly. Big wake-up call!

I knew this could not continue for long. Because of the restaurant I stayed until I felt really ready, to leave. It would be hard to let go of the restaurant, I felt resistance to that in me that I had to work out. I knew though that there was no other direction for our relationship except separation. I let myself get stronger in my reconnection to me first. That was my plan and strategy.

I decided it was time to do everything I could to empower myself, so I finally went for a healing with the friend of Christian. I had such a profound experience. I felt the energy flow into my body like a cascading waterfall, warm and nourishing. I wanted to do and know more. I asked if I could meet his teacher. He said she is booked a year in advance, that it wouldn't be likely. But I had a feeling I really needed to meet her and that I would.

After the session I went back to work; again Yuri had no interest in my experience and was as usual dismissive and grumpy.

I was getting to know one of our regular guests. Her name was Marcia, she was a healer and painter. She was there that night after my session. It was nice for me that she was there so I could have a conversation with someone who was connected to a deeper awareness of life.

I think she sensed what was happening in my relationship with Yuri which made her come more often. She was always engaging conversations about healing and empowerment.

One day at the restaurant she invited me to her studio to explore expressive painting as a way to move the energy in me toward healing. That sounded great to me. I started going to her studio a few times a week before my evening shift at the restaurant.

I had never painted with oils before, it was incredibly inspiring, exploring freestyle. My painting turned out more beautiful than I would have imagined. Spending time with her really built me up and strengthened my resolve to keep healing, learning, and doing what brings me joy. She also introduced me to the book by Louise Hay called *Heal Your Body*. It was about changing our inner dialogue, using positive affirmations to bring healing. It became my new bible.

One day when I had been walking to get something for the restaurant I took a different street than usual. I was looking in the storefront windows when I came upon a sign with a picture of a Native Elder on it. His name was Emaho. He was giving a talk and doing a ceremony the next day. I took the poster and decided I was going to go. I felt an energy of excitement course through me.

That night Christian came for dinner to the restaurant with some friends. One of them, Matthias, also knew the healer woman who was the teacher of Sebastian, the man I had the healing with. He told me he had learned with her too. Awesome! Christian shared he had recently gone to an open evening that she holds regularly for the first time, and offered that he could take me to the next one. Yes! Yes! Yes! I knew there had to be a way to meet her. It would be in two days time. Perfect! *Tomorrow Emaho, then the next day I would meet her*, I thought to myself with great excitement and joy.

In the coming days I also got a call from one of the dancers from Toronto that my teacher from Martial Dance was going to be teaching in Berlin at the end of the month. Wow! What a constellation of healing coming my way. I could feel life; Spirit was supporting me to grow out of the situation with Yuri and the restaurant. It was time to come back home to myself now that I had decided I deserve better and more. The universe was responding. It is a reciprocal universe, indeed. I was feeling it again. I was feeling me again.

Something my friend Fred in Thailand said to me in one our last conversations came back to me. "We are on a constant journey of remembering and forgetting. What happens eventually is we start remembering for longer periods of time, and forget less until we are whole." Yep, I had just come through a long phase of forgetting, but now I was remembering again. He had shared that quote with me so I could be more compassionate with myself and others. It worked.

The next night I went to see Emaho. From the picture that I saw on the poster he had a softness and deep compassion in his eyes. He had studied in Tibet for eight years with Tibetan Monks, and blended an integration of Native American teachings and Tibetan teachings to offer helpful reflections to those looking for deeper understanding of life and themselves.

When I heard him speaking, it all felt very familiar and very true. Though I do not remember the exact expressions that affected me, I remember feeling found. He was very wise and brought through a very smooth integration of life teachings that resonated deep in me.

It was a group of about 40 of us attending After his talk we waited as he got ready to do a Fire Dance with us where he places his hands in fire for a long period of time and transfers that energy and light of the fire into each of our bodies one by one for healing as we are dancing around him and the altar in a circle. The music was this amazing percussion with Tibetan mantras being sung in the back ground. It really put me into a healing meditative state. I was so happy to be there and I could feel myself growing and getting stronger every moment.

A few days after this amazing ceremony I was still feeling incredibly confident and grounded. I was also starting to push back a lot more, not letting his attempts to diminish me get to me. I could tell he was feeling frustrated that he was losing his power over me.

After work at the end of the night when we had just closed the restaurant, Yuri was in the kitchen while I was counting the money at the front. There was so much building tension since I had been branching out doing what I wanted to.

He approached me and criticized me for something, trying to make a dig at me. He said, "No wonder Emanuele didn't want to stay with you, you are too complicated!"

That used to be the Achilles heel that would break me; when Yuri would make a reference to Emanuele and me being complicated it was like a double whammy.

This time however, I sat up straight and I looked at him in the eyes and I said, "Yeah I am complicated and I like myself this way!"

Oh boy, did that ever tick him off. He went storming into the kitchen, cursing me. I sat there at the table and thought, Aha I got you, fully recognizing his manipulation strategies. "It's just a matter of time," I whispered under my breath. Just a matter of time. I still chuckle at the memory of his angry and powerless expression. As he marched into the kitchen. Triumph! I got him.

The day I had been eagerly waiting for finally came for me to meet this healer woman with Christian. I was so excited.

When I walked in the room and I saw her I felt like I knew her. She was German but she looked more Native American. She looked at me deeply and then smiled warmly. She had deep, clear compassionate eyes that made me feel instantly at ease and at home.

The room was set up with two massage tables in the center, there were about 30 people sitting around them. The purpose of this evening was for people who were wanting to inquire about the heart-light energy healing practice and experience a little bit of it on the table. Every one of us there would receive a mini-session. Awesome!

When it was my turn to get on the table, I was so nervous. The teacher, whose name was Hathor, was at the head of the table. When she put her hands over my eyes I felt this intense heat, like my whole body just went pop and opened. It was absolutely blissful. By the time I got off the table 10 minutes later I felt so altered and a little bit dizzy. Christian had to leave early unfortunately, so I had to leave with him even though I didn't want to.

As we were getting up to leave Hathor looked at me, seemingly questioning, *"where are you going?"* In my mind I said I have to go because he has to go. She looked at me a moment longer and then nodded her head and looked away. It was as if she had gotten confirmation of something and she knew something. That was my sense of it, anyway. I really hoped I could study with her one day.

Everything went on as usual at the restaurant for the rest of the month until my dance teacher came. I was remembering how amazing I felt doing the Martial Dance when I was in Toronto and couldn't wait to dance again with my teacher and some of the students who would come with him from Toronto for the workshop.

With all this new input in my life of these spiritual teachers and practices, I was reflecting a lot on my situation and how Yuri was able to manipulate me to the degree that I lost such touch with my soul's passions and love.

I came to the realization that he had been accessing my deepest core wounds through his diminishing comments. The wounds that had originated when I was a little girl, where I was rejected and bullied at school, which had compounded the same feelings I felt of being abandoned from my mom, then being teased by my sister and her friends.

I saw very clearly that because of that ancient and buried hurt inside me that had created the original distorted belief that there was something wrong with me as a child, was at the root of the subtle power he had over me. Like predators in the wild, they intuitively sense the weak ones of the herd, as he had sensed my weakness and vulnerability when we met.

Now a days we have the term Narcissistic Predator to define that abusive intent. Some narcissists are completely run by subconscious patterning that they developed to survive. They need to feel in power over someone to feel secure in their world. Other narcissists are aware of their actions and it is completely intentional.

I realized that it was inevitable that I would attract someone like Yuri. Whether it was him or someone else, I would have called that experience to me sooner or later, because it mirrored to me my foundational belief about myself. My patterns of feeling unlovable and not enough were a complete match to his patterns of needing to control and dominate someone who doesn't know their worth. What an awakening that was. It made perfect sense to me. I hadn't healed that childhood trauma yet, it was still buried deep inside me, so the unique constellation of what I was already healing and learning through from Thailand, my experience with Andre and family, then getting thrown out of Switzerland made me super vulnerable and the perfect prey.

I had been in the same kind of trauma trance that my puppy was in when he got attacked by the dog. Spinning in circles in myself, disoriented and confused, I had no solid ground in or under me. My identity was in flux. Perfect opportunity for someone like him to come in take advantage of the situation.

I was beginning to see the bigger purpose this experience with him and the restaurant and everything had for me. It was a doorway into myself so I could heal what wasn't in congruency with my heart and soul.

There is no happening without a reason but sometimes we have to dig deep and look deep in order to find it and understand. This was one of those situations. I couldn't remain a victim and come into my empowerment at the same time. I had to somehow look at what part of me enabled this to happen. Without blame, shame, or guilt. Just with pure compassionate observation of the facts and then clear actions to heal and remove myself from that situation.

I was so exhausted by the last four years turning me inside out and upside down, but I was still making it through, amazingly.

In retrospect the thought came to me that perhaps my numbness for the first year being with Yuri was my body saying, okay let's just take a break, let's just shut down for a while, stabilize into a routine, reboot, and just be here for a while because at that time that was the best option where I could actually land and pause to a certain degree.

Then when my system rebooted, I started coming back online in myself when I was ready. That feels really accurate to me, and makes so much sense. I would have been floating around otherwise, no papers, no direction, if I hadn't gone with him. I can see how that could very well have led to even worse situations. I may have just broken down and given up.

One night Mathias came in to the restaurant to tell me that Hathor was teaching the 1st degree in the Energy Work that coming weekend. The cells in my body leapt for joy! I can't begin to express the feelings that passed through me that moment. I told Yuri I was going. He created a big fuss but saw I wasn't budging from my choice. Being controlling as he was, he said he will drive me then, not Christian or Mathias, who had offered to.

I thought I could find my way to Hathor's but got lost. Yuri used that as another opportunity to tell me how incapable and stupid I was while driving around. I had a road map in my hand, found it and showed it to him.

He was just going on and on about my stupidity until we pulled up front of the her healing studio. I jumped out of the car, and yelled at him, "I am not stupid and I will find my own way home afterward." I slammed the door as loudly as I could, with all my power. Shaking and worked up, I went to the door where the training was happening. I knocked and she opened it, looking at me with warmth and what looked like a bit of concern. I was a few minutes late, so I apologized. She said no problem and I went in.

It was a two-day training with two attunements a day that open our capacity to tap in to healing frequencies. Attunements are like stabilizing your online connection to Spirit/God so you can channel this light energy to yourself as a practice of healing and self-actualization. It was a beautiful two days, I learned a lot.

I ended up studying with her for six years. Another blessing through having landed with Yuri. It is through that experience I came to know about her and find her. That practice became my foundational healing practice that had helped me so much, brought me through so many painful experiences. It is still my main self-healing practice.

Life is not a linear path, nor is the path of healing. We often need to go on these detours to be brought to the people and situations we otherwise wouldn't connect with. That's the power of the paradox. All experiences are useful to grow and learn from. In fact, without the contrast of duality, there would be nothing to catalyze new experiences or evolution at all. Life would be inert.

At the end of September I attended the workshop with my teacher from Toronto. As I knew it would, it moved me deeply and activated parts of me again that had been dormant too long.

Martial Dance can be very passionate, fiery, and really demands you be fully present in your body to catch even the slightest nuances of movement in your partner. It's about relationship; neither is the leader of the dance, you are tuning in to the movement patterns that are born between the two dancers from moment to moment, all improvised, and no music. It's incredibly profound.

Even though I was getting stronger and more independent, it was becoming really stressful with Yuri. He was continually trying to regain his former power over me, which led to a constant battle. Upon sharing my situation one night at class, one of my dancer friends from the Biodanza offered me her apartment.

She was going to be away for several months and said she was happy to help me out that way. I was so grateful for that. I moved out without telling him. Yuri had no idea where I was; he had to manage the restaurant on his own

I didn't have a lot of money, kindly, a friend of mine who owned a health-food store gave me food whenever I needed it, things that had gone off the expire date but were actually still good for a very long time after. She was so generous. I retreated into the apartment for the most part. It was nice not having to deal with the ever building tension and fighting with Yuri.

I took myself out for walks and went for coffee, things that I hadn't done by myself since I was with him. Even though I knew I needed to leave him completely, there were still these emotional webs or strings that would pull, that would make me question my decision. But I sensed those emotional fibers would quickly dissolve once there was complete separation.

Eventually I had to call him, because most of my belongings were in the apartment. As soon as he heard my voice he was gentle and loving and apologizing and wanting to know where I was, wanting to come see me right away, wanting to talk to me to make everything right.

I needed to get my things, so I agreed to meet. The sweet charismatic man I had met in the beginning was back. He seemed really wanting to make a change so that we could stay together. I hesitated, but because of those emotional strings, I said okay, let's try. After all, I'd invested every penny I should have earned in the restaurant. I figured I would at least give it one more try. But tI promised myself his would be the last time.

He was okay for a while but his controlling patterns started showing themselves within the week in little ways, and then after a few more weeks even more.

I finally said I can't do this anymore. I had to let him go and had to let the restaurant go. There was absolutely no other way for me to move forward. I didn't judge myself for going back. For the contrary, I felt I had really given it every chance possible and could now really be free. No more doubts.

I went back to my friend's place and Yuri closed the restaurant. He ended up gambling all the money away that I should have earned. My share in the restaurant was about $300,000 based on my working hours alone. It's ironic: it was the most money I had ever earned in my entire life and I didn't even get to see it or enjoy a penny of it. What a journey!

He thankfully decided he was going to go back to Indonesia but perhaps would return in a few months. I went with him to the airport to see him off and when he left I cried. I didn't understand why I cried so deeply because I was happy to be free. Those emotional fibers that bind us in unhealthy relationships can be tricky.

Now, reflecting, I think it was a release of my soul, not because I was sad. It was like the tears of the Olympian who had trained so hard and now finally achieved her goal and won; it was like my soul could finally breathe again.

When I went back to the apartment I found that he sold everything I could possibly have made some money off of.

I stood in the kitchen, laughing at the absurdity and audacity that he had to do that and just shook my head. My father came to my rescue and wired me some money to help me get back on my feet. Even though we had differences and he didn't understand me and my choices, he was always there for me when I needed help. Always. For that I am so grateful.

I started doing odd jobs like babysitting and I was also a dental assistant for a few weeks as well. It was a job a friend had hooked me up with, with their dentist friend.

Then one day I ran into an old guest from the restaurant, Samir, who owned a jewelry store not far from where the restaurant was, and he offered me a job to manage it. Wonderful. More blessings. I accepted and finally after a long time had a steady income again.

He sold really beautiful ethnic jewelry. Navajo silver and turquoise, also African and South American artifacts and jewelry. I loved it. Right up my alley. Since I had worked in sales from the age of 12 back home until I left when I was 18, it was perfect.

My first job when I was 12 was selling baby clothes at a local flea market. At 13 I got a job with the clothing chain Fairweather Canada where I was officially trained as a sales person. I was always the top sales person everywhere I worked. I had even maintained one shift a week during my punk phase.

I really enjoyed it, so I could easily take over the position he offered me.

Over the next months I was healing and regaining a sense of self. I spent a lot of time with Hathor; I went every week and made many new friends, both within her group in all the different dance groups I was a part of.

I was still reorienting myself. It had been a four-year marathon of one hard knock after the other, but I was getting stronger and learning how to navigate life again. When I look back, I see myself like the Energizer Bunny, I just kept on going. Which I see is a reason I made it through. I stayed in action. I used every opportunity I could to show up and keep re-embracing life again and again. But I was worn out inside and weary and I wanted to feel loved and important to someone. I still actually mourned the loss of connection with Emanuele. It still wasn't healed. I hadn't had the time to fully heal with everything that had followed. It would take time.

About five months later, I had let myself trust someone I had been getting to know over the last four months. He came into the jewelry store I worked in almost every day. We talked about metaphysical stuff and spirituality; actually he did more of the talking and I was an eager listener. We also went for walks sometimes, and for pizza once.

The things he spoke about were very thought-provoking and interesting, though at times I felt like it was twisting my brain a bit. Sometimes after a walk and talk with him I actually felt disoriented. I just attributed it to the far-out conversation.

One day he said something really odd while we were walking down the street. He asked me, "If we create our own reality why did you create me with this scar on my face?"

I was speechless, I had no idea what to say. My brain literally froze. So I just stayed silent and felt confused, because the way he said it was really weird, creepy almost.

There was a sharp edge to his voice, almost like suppressed anger and aggression. He made many strange comments like that that would unsettle me, where it catalyzed confusion and questioning of my reality and who I was. I told myself it was just me feeling awkward and uncertain because I had just come out of the abusive relationship. I didn't listen to my gut and inner nudges hat indicated something wasn't right about him. My own self-doubt blocked me from fully acknowledging those feelings.

I didn't catch on until it was too late that he was mentally ill and had been actually stalking me the whole time -- long before we met. Through his clever conversations, ever so slightly manipulating my mind each time, creating self-doubt in me, I didn't catch on to the trap I was heading into. He did it very skillfully, as only a psychopath can.

One morning, for the first time, I invited him in for tea. The night before I had gone dancing with a girlfriend Gabi at the Osho bar, he had been there too. When Gabi and I left at 6 in the morning he walked with us to the subway. I didn't think much of it until he got on the same train, so I asked him where he was going. He said he would walk me home. I said he didn't need to, I would be fine. He insisted to make sure I get home safely. Oh the irony of that.

When we arrived he had made a challenging remark at the door, "I bet you won't let me in for tea since you are so mistrusting," he said, with a crooked smile and an edge. It was true, I rarely let anyone in to my home. He knew this because I had told him that before. He often did that, made challenging remarks about me that would disarm me and somehow make me doubt myself, setting me up to feel I have to prove myself, that he is wrong about his judgements of me. Now I see he was intentionally baiting me.

Instead of following my gut, my ego that wanted to prove there was nothing wrong with me. I took the bait. I invited him in.

Shortly after entering my home, he raped me. He held me at knife point and psycho-terrorized me the whole day. I was lucky to make it out alive.

I realized at one point that to keep freaking out, as I was doing, would aggravate him even more, and he was just waiting for me to totally lose it, to take a knife to him or something that would give him the go-ahead to finish me off. He was taunting me to take the knife from him, to stop him.

I was pinned against and was praying like crazy, repeating 'God Bless" over and over hundreds of times when a thought came to me to pretend like nothing happened. *"Use Reverse psychology"*, I heard in my thoughts.

His psycho-mind terror was worse than the actual rape. I just wanted him out. So I took that thought-advice and did just that. He removed the knife from my throat eventually, staring me down with the darkest glare you can imagine when he realized I wasn't going to fight back.

He started making all these demands, to sit down beside him and kiss him on the cheek, that maybe then he will go, pointing his finger at to his cheek. And other really peculiar demands like to make him toast with honey, and showing me how I should spread it on the toast with love, and that I should feed it to him. I complied without resistance. I then had a shower and went to the kitchen and pretended like nothing happened and washed the dishes.

He gradually came out of his psychopathic state. He entered the kitchen and started telling me about his childhood in Columbia, the war and its effects and other stuff I don't remember now. I pretended I was really listening; *"Hmm, that must have been hard,"*, I said. That went on for about 15-20 more minutes, I just kept busy cleaning, moving stuff around. Trying to figure out how to get him out of my home.

Then at one point I said quite plainly and matter of fact, "You know, a friend is waiting for me, I have to go now." I grabbed my bike and opened the door that he had previously slammed on my foot when I tried to get away. I moved swiftly and stepped into the hallway. Once I was out the door he had no choice but to follow. He came out, and I locked the door.

He glared at me and in the most evil way imaginable and said, "You got me out!" I said, "Yes I did!" with strength in my voice. He then said, "No you didn't. I am in you now more than ever!"

"Oh no you are not." I said with all the inner strength I could muster. I took off on my bike and rode for as long as I felt it would take for him to be gone.

When I got home, I showered again, scrubbed my body, wrote my whole experience out, did a ceremony and I prayed to understand what I needed to heal so that I didn't attract that kind of manipulation and abuse ever again. I asked for help to heal what blocks me from trusting my gut in those kinds of situations. In other situations, I was always great and in tune, my gut instincts were clear. But in this regard, in this context, of subtle manipulative abuse, my discernment mechanism was not working well. The sexual abuse I experienced as a child had disrupted my capacity to discern and I would just freeze.

I finished my ceremony, I drummed and sang for a bit and then called Heiri. He gave me the number of his shaman teacher Leah who I had met a few times before. She counseled me, said it wasn't my fault. I just need to find and heal my blind spot. She told me to be gentle with myself. I cried so much.

Talking with her helped a lot. Then I phoned my friend Thomas who I had stayed with in my first months in Berlin and asked him if he would stay with me for a while so I wasn't alone. He came over right away. Such a good friend.

I needed to get out of Berlin. Heiri made the offer to go work for his mother. Two weeks later I left for Switzerland. I got the work visa easily so clearly enough years had gone by that I was allowed to go back in. Thank God for that! I don't know what I would have done otherwise.

I started working at Heiri's mothers restaurant in a small mountain village. It was a beautiful location but it turned out to not be an easy time either. I had hoped for a nourishing and healing experience there, but it was the exact opposite. Something about me triggered his mother constantly. She was a real tyrant with me, I could do nothing right in her eyes. My sense is she was jealous about my friendship with Heiri and other things about me too.

She and her daughters became progressively really abusive towards me. I didn't understand why and after having gone through everything I had just come through it really broke me. They even turned Heiri against me while I was there.

Once again, I found myself alone and isolated. One day I spoke with one of the waitresses who had lived and worked there for many years about what was happening. She told me that all three of them always picked someone each year that they treated as they did me, to not take it personally.

Easier said than done, but knowing that it wasn't just me did make it a bit easier to navigate. It is in my time there that I received my education about projections, how people project their subconscious junk on others to avoid seeing themselves, and about passive-aggression. It was actually very enlightening in the end.

I felt very alone and cried a lot in my room after each shift. But I was away from Berlin and thanked God I was in a beautiful mountain paradise, so I could retreat into Nature any time. That helped a lot.

I also had reconnected with a friend named Elvira in a neighboring village that I met through Heiri a few years before. We became really good friends. She had a spiritual oriented life too and she owned a dance studio. What a bonus that was! I would rent it from her at least once a week to just dance my body and soul free. We also went on regular walks together. She was an angel that helped me through that time.

One day an acquaintance that I had met through the restaurant brought me to a hidden waterfall; only the locals knew about its location.

When we arrived there was a man sitting on the edge of the small cliff with a bottle of wine and a crystal wine glass, just enjoying himself in that beautiful place. *So cool,* I thought. What an interesting person; I felt drawn to him. We ended up talking a bit. It turned out he was from Canada. Of all places, eh! Again sweet serendipities creating magic in my life.

We became good friends that summer, he was my saving grace in so many ways. One person, in a sea of strangers who had all abused, misunderstood, and misperceived me. He saw me and my heart. I have absolutely no idea what I would have done or how I would have survived without his friendship.

Even though I did feel an attraction to him, but because of the rape experience, I was totally shut down in that area. In the first period of getting to know each other I was quite paranoid and anxious, not sure if I could trust my instincts.

He was kind and understanding and never demanded or pushed for more than friendship, even though I knew he felt more for me and hoped for more intimacy one day. That kindness led me to open my heart and trust his intentions were honorable.

He would pick me up and take me to beautiful nature spots on my days off and often would also pick me up after work to go to this amazing dance place that was called Ugly, just a few towns from where I worked. I would dance my sorrows away until the wee hours of the morning. Then we would go for a bite to eat at 5:30 a.m. at this great Swiss restaurant, *Marche*, that was open 24, hours before he would bring me back to the restaurant, where I lived in a room above it.

I was still playing my little bamboo flute every time I went into Nature. He was one of the first people to hear me play, actually. He really appreciated my love of Nature and whenever I felt an urge to stop somewhere to play he would always stop driving and park for me so I could.

I saw one of the most beautiful rainbows in my life while we were driving by a lake one day. He stopped for me and I lingered there playing until the rainbow disappeared. It was pure magic. His kindness helped me heal a lot, I was still so fragile and just starting to rebuild myself, again!

One day I brought him to this amazing store in Rappersville that Heiri had introduced me to. It was in a small town about an hour away, where they sold Native American crafts and flutes. I had been there a few times before, each time admiring the flutes. This time that day I found a flute that spoke to me and decided I was going to save to buy it. It was $900 Swiss francs. I was thrilled and couldn't wait until I had enough to get it.

One night after another challenging day at the restaurant, Peter picked me up to go for a bite to eat. I sat in the car and all of a sudden he extended his right hand in front of me, holding the flute I wanted to buy. I was speechless.

He said, "You are worth it!" and he gave it to me.! Just like that. This flute became my medicine to heal. It helped me to bring out all the emotions and feelings that were in my body, soul, and being that no words could express. It became both my call to prayer and my answer.

A month later I finished my season there not a second too soon. It got really crazy in the end, I was so happy to get out of there. It was all I could do to get through the day. The hostility and aggression that came my way everyday was brutal.

In my time there I had discovered this singer from Lapland named Marie Boine. The music is very earthy and primal, with her powerful voice. Every morning I would look in the mirror, assure myself that I can make it through the day, that I am worthy of love and I am good enough, even if they didn't see it.

I would take several deep breaths, then, I would play one specific song by Marie Boine that made me feel empowered and I would belt it out at the top of my longs. It was my warrior song. It helped.

Peter and I had ended up parting ways shortly before I left. His feelings had grown for me to the point he wanted more in the end, and I couldn't give him that. A part of me wished I could but I was nowhere near ready for it.

In that last month I had also become friends with the owner of the flute store. Her name was Bettina It was lovely chatting and spending time with her when I could. I would take the bus and train to Rappersville every week to visit. Sometimes she would visit me too.

She picked me up after my last shift and gave me a ride all the way to my stepfathers home in Bonndorf Germany. That was so nice of her.

As we left the restaurant Heiri's mother practically chased me out yelling at me. It was absolutely unreal! Bettina laughed at the outrageousness of this woman.

I don't know if we had past life karma or who I reminded her of that triggered her so much. It was also like because I had learned to not react to her treatment of me as I had done in the beginning before I understood about projections, it frustrated her even more. She wanted to battle and I wouldn't give it to her. That made her even more furious with me. What learnings that provided me with! Incredible.

Rheinhold received me with great love Dear Rheinhold, such an amazing man. Even though my mother had left him, he still insisted I was his daughter no matter what. Such a beautiful soul he was, I am forever grateful for his love and presence in my life.

I stayed with him for a few weeks, then went back to Berlin. I had sublet my apartment the six months I was away. I was nervous about going back.

My boss at the jewelry store said I still had my job if I wanted it, so I worked for a few months and also babysat for some friends as an extra job. I also got a part time job in a Canadian Coffee Shop that was a lot of fun with great people.

In that time, I continued to do my dance classes, doing Biodanza and Five Rhythms and Energy Work evenings, until I gave up my apartment just before Christmas to go back to visit my family in Toronto.

I had no idea what would come next; I just knew I needed to leave everything behind for a while, to get in touch with my roots and wait for the next nudge to lead me.

I returned to Toronto until March. I did a few odd jobs while I was there and spent time with Gennie and my other friends too. It was a time of deep pause and restoration. Then one day I felt the nudge to return to Berlin and start over. My soul did not feel at home in Ontario, and it was still challenging for me with my family.

Samir helped me find a new apartment in a cool area of Berlin, in Kreuzberg. I got my old job back at *Barcomi's,* the Canadian Coffee House, and at Samir's store.

This is when my cycle of hard knocks of the past four years paused and a restorative time of healing began for me for the next four years. I rose and I conquered and healed many layers. It was an amazing four year cycle of empowerment, healing, growth, joy and deep friendships.

In those four years back in Berlin, it was like a rebirth of my heart and soul. I gathered many tools to heal myself that helped me so much. I continued studying energy healing with Carol, ultimately being initiated as a teacher.

The Energy Work got me through so much, it's a gift for me to now be able to share this empowering healing technique. I also continued dancing, exploring Shamanism and kept learning with Emaho until the end of those four years when the next nudge came and I left Berlin for British Columbia.

All the teachers and mentors that I continued learning with in those years cultivated so much understanding of myself and my emotional patterns, enabling me to intentionally direct healing into my life. I was ready for something new. A new adventure.

EPILOGUE

WHERE I AM NOW AND
HOW I GOT HERE

"No experience has been too slight,
and the least incident unfolds like a destiny,
and fate itself is like a wonderful wide web in
which each thread is guided
by an infinitely tender hand,
and laid alongside another and held and
borne up by a hundred others."
– Rainer Marie Rilke

In those 4 years in Berlin, as I mentioned, I had come to a place of great joy and confidence again in a way that I had never known before, and I had so many friends to share my life with. It was truly a golden era for me. There are many stories and adventures that would fill another book, maybe even two, but needless to say the magic and serendipities continued and I healed so much.

Unbeknownst to me, those four years were actually strengthening and preparing me for the deep dive that was about to happen when I decided to move back to Canada at the end of that four year period.

Yes, I had uncovered and gained understanding of many of the root causes for several of the subconscious belief systems that were revealed from those traumatic experiences, but I hadn't yet engaged the wounds these beliefs supported and created completely at their depth.

Those four years in Berlin were like a reprieve where I could regain a sense of self and balance that deeply nourished me and my connection to life and universal forces of Light and Good.

Sometimes I feel as if I have lived a dozen lives in this one life! What a glorious and intricate tapestry this life has been and is! I am beyond grateful to have grown and healed into the person I am today. For me it is a miracle.

My life was so amazing and full in Berlin, but at one point I felt an inner restlessness and got the inner nudge that it was time to leave Germany. My time there felt done, I had reached a point that I could not envision my future there anymore.

I had no idea what I was going to do or where I was going to go, I just knew Germany was over. It was getting harder to get my working visa each time I applied, which was frustrating, and kept me in fear of 'what if' they don't renew it.

Even though my mother was German born, she was apparently born in the wrong year for it to give me residency. I was also getting tired of the restaurant industry and wanted to focus more on doing massage and healing.

One day I found out through a friend that my elder Emaho was doing a retreat in Scotland in two weeks-time. What perfect timing, right in the precise moment when I was questioning what I would do! My gut instincts said to go to the retreat, so I did, even though my finances were very low. When it comes to healing and gaining clarity my motto is all or nothing! I trusted I would be fine and taken care of as I always had been. I booked my ticket and off I went!

I saw Emaho in the airport when I arrived in Scotland, it was so nice seeing him again. When he asked how I was doing I shared with him that I sensed my current life was shifting but I didn't know where to. He grinned and said, "You will know by the end of the retreat." *Wow! Ok!* I thought, *I hope that's true.* It turned out he was right!

Three nights before the retreat completed I heard in my dreams "move to Vancouver"... three times in a row! I woke up in the morning and thought about it for a moment. I didn't know much about Vancouver. *Hmm...*I thought... *there's the ocean, there are forests and there are mountains...I can do that! Perfect!*

When I told Emaho later that day he agreed it was the perfect place for me. In the remainder of my time in Scotland, as serendipity would have it, I met someone who lived in Vancouver and she offered for me to stay with her and her son until I got things sorted out. Wow! This Universe is truly amazing.

At the end of the retreat I returned to Berlin, and immediately the next day I booked a flight for three months later. I liquidated my belongings, packed and shipped what I wanted to bring with me, got on the plane and then just showed up. Another new beginning.

When I arrived in Vancouver I was beaming; full of light, enthusiasm, and so much joy and hope for the life I wanted to create -- only to experience feeling misunderstood and emotionally squashed repeatedly, again and again starting with the woman I was staying with. It was a real mystery for me. I was so loved in Germany! What happened?

I was first so completely misperceived by her, and with such volatility it was quite frightening She had shared with me something she was struggling with that I, with all my heart, offered some thoughts that could potentially help her find a solution. She freaked out, called me arrogant and even called Emaho telling him that I was trying to be her teacher, which I wasn't at all, I was sharing with genuine care because I saw her suffering. This created a rift between me and Emaho. I didn't feel seen and I no longer felt safe sharing with him because he didn't take the time to check out my end of the experience, he just took what she said at face value and, according to her, he said I was wrong to have said anything at all. That really hurt. Through her irrational interpretation and behaviour I lost a mentor who I had trusted and who had helped me so much in the previous years.

Then, like dominos, I had many more experiences of triggering people. I had no idea why. It was so confusing for me the amount of rejection I was encountering.

I later came to understand that a big part of being misunderstood was cultural differences. Without my realizing it I had become more German in my ways of thinking and relating, which means I was very direct and forthright and that I was also very engaging.

When a friend in Germany would talk about a problem, with all sincerity and my whole heart, I would offer new possibilities of thought or action that could potentially help them, as my friends there did with me. My experience in Germany and Switzerland, when friends share a problem, it is an automatic invitation to sleuth solutions and possibilities that we may not yet see with them. Sharing problems was about finding new actions and solutions to make things better.

It took a while, and many rejections later, that I observed that a good majority of the people I met only wanted to talk about their problems and remain a victim of them, and in turn resented me for even suggesting a solution. I was often reprimanded *"who do you think you are?"* I was also told I was arrogant and self-centred many times, completely contradictory to how I knew myself and where I was coming from in my communications. I was apparently just supposed to listen and agree. It was the complete opposite to how I had learned to be in Germany. I could also tell that the depth of my spiritual approach to life either irritated people or it made them dismiss me as a dreamer or New Age weirdo. It's quite funny actually when I think of it now.

Another element contributing to being misunderstood, I was also needing to learn how to express myself in English after years of communicating in German, a language that has such immense capacity to express even the slightest nuance of thought and feeling. Since I had left home when I was 18, my formative years were in Europe and Asia. I felt so inept to express myself in English, which was so surprising considering it is my birth language.

Those dynamics, amongst some other challenging and hurtful experiences that happened in my first years in BC, eventually it wore me down and overwhelmed me and my capacity to navigate. I plummeted into depression, which brought me to meet the core layers of my most painful cherished wounds of feeling unloved and excluded. Even in the so-called spiritual communities I temporarily engaged there was so much passive aggression, entitlement and judgement. I had nowhere to land and rest, nowhere and no one I could feel safe with, so I completely withdrew.

This was however another hidden blessing. In my withdrawing, my deep-rooted subconscious beliefs that I was not loveable and not good enough could come forward for me to see and engage. Though my new environment didn't reflect the light and goodness of my heart back to me as I experienced in Germany, it did fully mirror those diminishing beliefs back to me in high definition.

There is a Sanskrit expression that I love so much that it makes me chuckle every time I think of it, because it gives a clear reflection of how we generally go through life and move on from painful experiences in order to 'get over it'. It goes like this, "The elephant got through the door but the tail got stuck." Think about it.

It's so funny and so true. To survive we push through the big stuff and layers just enough so we can move forward and on with our lives, as I had done. That's the big elephant who got through the door.

The tail ends that get stuck are the deeper layers of emotional pain that are too overwhelming to feel and process, so they get left behind. We bury them, ignore them, we numb them out, we pretend they don't exist and build coping mechanisms to keep them buried and hidden. We stuff them in our *"emotional backpack"* where they collect until the weight is too heavy to bear and our body and our soul one day finally say *"Enough!"*

From time to time these tail ends show themselves as uncontrolled reactions, triggers, temporary emotional meltdowns that we later dismiss as a mood or something else.

The thing is, it is always more than that and until we take the time to look deeper we suffer. In order to be a happy and thriving human being we have to go all the way into our pain and emotional shadows in order to gain knowledge of them and heal what is hiding in our subconscious. Otherwise our subconscious and all its misinformed beliefs and stories run the show.

As I was doing my best to figure out what was happening I also remembered something Carol said to me when she initiated me as a teacher, which rang true as another layer of what I was experiencing. She said that this path of being a healer and teacher is not for the faint of heart and that I will be even more sensitive to perceiving subtleties and energy. She told me that there is a reason why in the old days the healers and wisdom carriers lived at the outer edges of the villages, that as the saying goes *'a prophet is never recognized in their own country and are often prosecuted'*, as healers are rarely embraced where they live. People are mostly afraid of the unknown and are very uncomfortable with change, so they make their own stories to stay comfortable and not have to question their world and beliefs. That I may be alone in my life a lot for that reason.

She also expressed that this journey of healing and self-realization is not for everyone and that it is the hardest path we can choose because it will bring us face to face with ourselves, shadows and all. *But*, she said, it is the most fulfilling and rewarding path we can take.

Her words carried me through many moments for sure as I attempted to navigate my new environment. I definitely felt very out of place and out of sync with the collective energy and psychology of where I was.

What I also came to understand through both Carole and Emaho is that many people will react negatively to someone who is actively engaged in their own healing, who are in a momentum of transformation and growth, because it triggers the tail ends that they have buried in their subconscious that they do not want to see. I reminded myself of that as often as I could. It helped me make some sense of some of what I was experiencing.

In those first years in Vancouver I found myself getting emotionally high-jacked by trauma triggers, so often that my self-esteem dropped drastically. My buoyant spirit dimmed. I was so confused. I could not understand why I could not retain and access my joy and higher knowing that I was otherwise connected to anymore.

Because of my healing experiences in Berlin where I felt I had reclaimed my empowerment and joy after healing so much I had thought I was done, I had thought I had gone as deep as I needed to.

Nope. Not quite yet. In reality, I had really just done the prep work for the deep, dark and beautiful descent into the innermost unexplored caverns of my heart and soul.

When I reflect back to my sweet naivety of thinking that I was 'done' I am reminded of one of my favorite and humorously humbling poems by a Persian poet named *Hafiz*.

"It is always a danger to aspirants on the path, when they begin to believe and act as if the ten thousand idiots who so long ruled inside, have all packed their bags, skipped town, or died!"

Our unconscious trauma patterns that cause us to act out in dysfunctional and harmful ways are the ten thousand idiots, so to speak There is so much wisdom in that poem. It is a reminder to be humble and know that everyone of us has our 'idiots inside' that make us blind and act without reason. They don't just up and leave just like that, it takes time and commitment to our healing before they no longer affect us. We heal in layers, not all at once. As long as we are human, we are never done.

It was also really hard for me to find work in Vancouver. Everywhere I applied I was told I was over qualified for every job. I even went to the Welfare office where I was treated so horribly that when I left there I said to myself there is no way I am going back there. Through them though I got connected to a work agency that focused in the Hospitality Industry. Though I really didn't want to do that work anymore it was a place to start.

One night just a few days after getting my resume done with the agency I opened a spiritually oriented magazine to the classified page and I found an ad for a fishing lodge looking for someone to set up a spa on it for them.

I was already so beaten down by my first six months I prayed so hard to get the job. Which I gratefully did! I saw a glimmer of hope and light in my future with that opportunity. It seemed perfect until it wasn't anymore. Living in total isolation like that with strangers, most at least a decade younger than me, it was like the reality show Survivor. I made the best out of it I could, but it was so hard.

As one the cooking staff said to me, as I was struggling to find my way there with all the gossip and stuff that went on, 'you are an enigma, you are different, and people don't like different, they attack it, especially in this kind of environment'. Boy was she right!

Nonetheless I did my job, and I did it well, the Spa was a great success, but my relationships with the staff were seriously wanting. They were really mean spirited with me because I was so different. I avoided contact with the them as much as I could. It was a very painful experience for me, but again at the same time, it taught me a lot. I went back for the second season more aware and equipped to navigate and had a better time. Again, each one of them played their perfect role rejecting me for me to learn what I needed to learn, to not give power and authority to others over me and that I do not need to prove myself. I can be just me, and I can let them be them.

In the process though of figuring this out, with everything else I was going through trying to adjust culturally, plus some other situations, created the perfect inner storm that left me feeling completely lost.

Rejection and feeling excluded was my Achilles tendon. It was my kryptonite! It could drop me in a nano-second. The wounds born from the abandonment of my mother all those years ago, and the bullying in school was reactivated in my nervous system full throttle!

Who knew we could carry so much beneath the outward lives we live. I sure didn't, but we do. We all do. That is another of our common threads that unites us.

I was brought to my knees. I felt like I had travelled back in time. I questioned all the healing I had thought I had experienced and the wisdom and understanding I thought I had attained. I felt like I had no access to any of it at all.

I found myself on another inner pilgrimage from Ben to Benah. My limbic system went into fight or flight mode and it felt like I was back at the beginning. I found myself feeling dissociated and fearful of life and people again, but with a new tone of bitterness that caused emotional volatility to arise in me at times whenever I felt misunderstood, deceived or abused passive aggressively. In the past I would just shrink back. Now I started fighting back.

I didn't know myself anymore. I was desperately grasping on to the memories of myself before these experiences that broke me happened.

It took about two years after all those experiences to heal through the thick of it and several more years reconnecting to my heart and piecing the fragments of my life together to restore my buoyancy and joy and cultivate a state of wholeness in me again.

All of this has taught me that until we heal our hidden hurts and traumas, they emit a frequency that makes us a magnet to keep attracting the same scenarios again and again until we finally learn and heal. It's our own personal Ground Hog Day, like the movie with Bill Murray. The Law of Resonance and Attraction is real and is at play every moment of our existence, with every thought we have and every action, and every subconscious pain that is vibrating and attracting the people and situations to trigger it so we can finally heal.

I went on to study many healing modalities in the following years that brought me healing and I received some Shamanic Healing with an elder who did Plant Spirit Medicine, which was very effective. I also sang in his powwow drum circle, I love singing, this brought me great joy. And of course, I spent a lot of time in Nature. All of this helped me land in my self again thankfully. I showed up for every opportunity to learn and heal, that is what got me through. Had I become stagnant and inactive, I never would have made it.

Though my start here in BC was hard, to say the least, I have to say it was absolutely perfect! My school of hard knocks has opened me to know myself and life so deeply in ways that would not be possible otherwise. It has also grown my capacity for compassion towards others immensely.

"Pain is the cracking of the shell that enfolds your understanding"
- Kahlil Gibran

That statement is so true. I believe that this quote that I read the night before I departed for Germany in the book I mentioned earlier, *The Prophet*, was like a seed that got planted in the earth of my soul, that it sprouted and nourished me with wisdom my entire life thereafter. That observation of giving a purpose to pain gave me strength, courage and hope.

I actually have gratitude for all those who challenged and rejected me. They played their role perfectly in my life to bring my wounds to the surface and help me grow. I am also very grateful to those who saw me beyond what I was processing, that didn't label, dismiss or conclude me to something less than I was. They saw through the outer appearance of chaos that was forming a butterfly. They saw my heart and soul completely. To those of you who saw my inner light, you contributed to my healing immensely. You know who you are if you are reading this.

The Nature of British Columbia was the perfect healing refuge for me. Always my saving Grace! Being so close to the ocean mountains and forests nourished me as always. My forever refuge. I also recognize that if I would have stayed in Germany, I likely would never have gotten to the core of my traumas because I needed to feel absolutely safe, which as a foreigner there is always that shaky feeling of what if? I needed to be in my country where I have rights, where I can't get kicked out of, where I could finally rest and unwind all that had been built up in my nervous system all those years. Though there were times I seriously questioned my choice to move to BC, it was indeed the best place for me.

I had the blessing of someone I met when everything fell apart, a complete stranger, who after a few conversations sensed the goodness in my heart, my commitment to heal and my desperate need for the time and space to do so. He offered to help me financially for a year or as long as I needed so I could do my inner work to get my feet back on the ground. What an incredible Blessing that was.

In that time period I took part in a Vision Quest. A Vision Quest is when you go up a mountain and find a space that you are drawn to where you stay alone for four days and nights to pray and call in your vision or guidance, with no food and no water. An elder remains at a camp below and comes to check on you twice a day. It was quite an intense healing experience. The elder running this Vision Quest revealed to me just before I went up to my spot that my nervous system was compromised by Post Traumatic Stress Disorder. At that time in my life I had no idea what that was or what it meant except that war veterans experienced it. As she explained it to me it opened my eyes a lot and gave me a new focus to direct my reflections and healing in the coming days. I felt transformed when I came down on the fifth morning. It was amazing. Half way through I didn't think I would make it, but I did. Prayer is powerful medicine.

After the Vision Quest I wanted to learn as much as I could about trauma as I could. The more I learned, the more I came to understand myself. It was so liberating to have an explanation for those moments when I would sometimes get so hijacked by debilitating emotions that it would shut me and my heart down. This is when my healing gained great momentum.

Again, there are many more journeys and stories in the years that followed as my healing journey continued bringing me to who and where I am now.

The magic and adventure continued as an active force in my life. I consistently dedicated myself to learning as much as possible to understand both my biology and my spirituality. I studied everything I could get my hands on about PTSD, how our brains work, how we can rewire them, our body chemistry, Quantum Physics, Esoteric Sciences, you name it I was studying up on it to know myself better. I discovered Peter Levine's book *Awakening the Tiger: Healing Trauma,* which became like my bible and gave me the tools to navigate my nervous system with greater awareness and self-care. What many don't realize is that Post Traumatic Stress is not caused just by extreme events. It is a spectrum, and the majority of people have PTSD in varying degrees. Anywhere we have felt our safety threatened, where we had to shrink ourselves to survive an abusive influence in our lives, where there was not enough love to balance it out, our nervous system has been traumatized and carries the charge of the memory until we heal it and rewire ourselves.

In the following years I succeeded in rewiring my brain and nervous system to the point where former trauma reactions that once ruled me no longer do. Now I can consciously chose my responses. What a spectacular difference that has made all the difference in my life.

This is why I have been moved to write this book and share my story. Even if only one person reads it and is inspired to keep on living and building a better life, it has served it's purpose.

When I share some of my story with female clients that are looking for healing and reclaiming their life after trauma and they see where I am in my life now, they feel hope that they too can heal. They see and know that I am very familiar with the territory they are in, they see I have walked the trenches they are caught in and I come out victorious. This allows them to open and trust. They see it is truly possible to heal that it is possible to rise out of the depths of depression and anxiety and create a fulfilling life.

As I have come to understand trauma, our nervous system never forgets, it's not supposed to, it stores the memories to give us signals intended to protect us when needed.

Though we cannot erase the trauma memories in our nervous system, we can however learn to navigate and redirect our reactions to the triggers when they occur, so we do not get taken down by them by destructive behavior. We can basically create new neuro-pathways to navigate the trigger moments better, so we do not harm ourselves or others.

That is the journey of self-mastery that has defined me and my life in the coming years and that continues in every moment today. Mastery is not something you just arrive at and your done. Every level of Mastery we attain opens to another level, and another level, like in video games.

When I had originally felt that inner nudge to move to Vancouver, I had imagined only easy and good times. There is a quote that comes to mind: *"I seldom arrive where I intended to go – but always ended up where I needed to be."*

It is truly magical how things happen. Had I even had an inkling of an insight that I would go through so much pain I probably would not have moved here! It's quite humorous actually! I am chuckling out loud as I write this.

I feel like my soul guided me in ways my mind could never have fathomed or figured out. I needed to only envision the best in order to get me to move into the unknown as I did.

This choice to move here also ultimately led me to Hawaii, through a chance meeting with someone on Galiano Island, (another magical journey).

As I shared in the Introduction when I was in Hawaii I was blessed to learn many deep healing principles, practices and understandings that affirmed everything that I learned from nature and my heart so completely. I found the home of my soul in Hawaii.

I am even more honored and blessed to have been initiated as Kumu and Kahu, Teacher and Healer, of these practices and wisdoms, initiated by my dear friend and Kahuna Elder Harry Uhane Jim.

Over the years I have often wondered why and how I have always experienced such a deep intuitive knowledge of Nature and Spirit and why I always felt such a strong connection to all Aboriginal and Earth based Traditions and Wisdoms that I have encountered.

Recently some pieces of my ancestry came together for me that make a lot of sense and grounds me even more in the awareness of the Power of Nature that has guided me and why I have had it. Aside from my Elders telling me I have been Hawaiian and Native American in many lives, I have discovered another reason.

I am a Heinz variety, with a very diverse multi-cultural genetic heritage. The one that stands out most for me right now is my Nordic Ancestors, the Celts and Vikings. Not many realize the teachings of Mother Earth that these people carry are pretty identical to all the teachings of Mother Earth from all Tribal and Aboriginal peoples in the world.

When we view the Old Europeans, our perception generally only takes us as far back as the Aristocrats and Religious Orders that violently harmed so many people and cultures in the world. That is how I have viewed them, and I always felt ashamed of what some of my genetic ancestors were a part of.

But when we go further back in time, we find a people that were deeply connected to the wisdoms of the Earth, the Pagans, Druids, Celts, and Vikings. Most of these nature loving wise peoples were killed during the time of the Inquisition, an estimated nine million. It is no wonder those wisdoms got buried and lost, there was hardly anyone still alive to bring them forward.

The spiritual wisdoms I discovered recently of Nordic Clans, are remarkably similar to all that I learned from Nature and my Elders, both Native American and Hawaiian.

They honor the Energy and Spirit of each direction, they connect to the elements of nature, Earth, Water, Fire, Air, and Animal Spirits, recognizing these elements as mirroring the same elements in us. They sing and drum in the same way, they honor all life as sacred, For them Nature was/is where we can directly experience "God".

You know how something can be staring you in the face but you don't see it until you're ready to? I knew about Paganism, that's how my inner journey was first nourished and I have known for a while that I have Viking and Celtic heritage, but I never until now put the two together. It all makes perfect sense to me now.

Though it clearly skipped several generations, my Ancient Nordic and Celtic genetics were awoken in my life. The way I sing, The way I drum, the way I play the flute, my connection to Nature suddenly makes more sense to me than ever before I always felt a bit weird in my twenties and thirties because of my deep spiritual inclinations. In my forties I have claimed my uniqueness and accepted I am not everyone's cup of tea but still couldn't fully place why I have this activated deep connection to Nature as I do. And now, how beautiful it is that these realizations of my ancestry have come to me as I am finishing this book. For me it just brings it all together. I can't even express in words this new found inner strength and connection I feel to my-self and my ancestors now. I see how knowing our genetic roots is really important to knowing and understanding ourselves.

My heart adheres to the teachings of Mother Earth that are the Universal teachings of Spirit/God. These teachings are inclusive, not exclusive. These teachings do not belong to any man, religion or tradition, in the same way the Earth cannot belong to anyone. These teachings are available to every willing and open soul who seeks them. Though of course the rituals vary from continent to continent, tribe to tribe and are unique in every way, I see that the essence behind them is the same and in order to go beyond our differences and defenses, acknowledging that sameness is essential.

My heart tells me that unless we start meeting each other in that awareness of the essence behind all Traditions and Religions, with openness and inclusiveness, focusing on the common threads that unite us, where we can meet from a place of soul rather than personality, truth rather than dogma, nothing can ever change in the violent dynamics we see happening every day in our communities and the world. The Human drama will continue and escalate until we stop letting our traumas lead our perceptions, so we can finally heal. If we don't choose to let our higher Good/God nature lead us, both individually and globally, there is no way we can recover from the results of our traumas that are visible everywhere we look. We need to heal.

I would like to take this moment to express my immense gratitude to the Native Aboriginal Elders and Hawaiian Elders that, through their own healing and rising above the pain and wounds of history, opened their wisdoms and culture to me.

Had those wisdoms and practices not been opened to me, I would surely not be here today. That is for certain. I would have taken my life long ago. Those teachings were my stronghold in my darkest moments.

I owe my life to the love and wisdoms of Mother Earth that I was always connected to, that were confirmed to me through the Elders that Graced and Blessed my life.

Perhaps it is time for us to go deeper into our roots in the West and connect to our ancient spiritual heritage. To connect in Unity as Souls rather than keep creating exclusions based on differences that don't necessarily need to divide us. To come together as a Global Family, The Rainbow Tribe that was prophesized by the Hopi Elders long ago. We need to reconnect to our Mother, now more than ever, before we destroy all that is Good, that is Love in ourselves and the world.

"Out beyond the ideas of right doing and wrong doing'
There is a field.
I will meet you there"
- Rumi

I would like to posit a possibility, if you will.

What if we could see that every human being is carrying the traumas of centuries of humanities misinformation, misdeeds, violence and confusion? Because we all do.

What if we can see how those traumas and their effects connect us in an inexplicable way? A way that can lift us out of the barbaric battles of who is right and who is wrong, and that can lead us to understanding, to mutually looking for a way to heal together?

What if we live knowing that the color of our skin, our culture and countries, our orientations in life, all the things that we use to divide us, can actually inspire and enhance us?

Nature thrives when there is diversity. Since we are Nature it seems reasonable to me that the same applies to us. My life is so much richer because of all the cultures and different people from different walks of life I have encountered.

I know based on where we are currently, it sounds impossible and altruistic, but if we don't have something to focus on and somewhere to start at least, a new thought or possibility to create an new path that can bring good to ourselves, our relationships and the world, how can we create the world peace we all say we want?

Pono-Effectiveness is the measure of Truth. If that is so, which makes perfect sense to me, I think we can all agree that the way we have been doing things till now is in no way effective to supporting life to continue, nor creating Love, Peace and Unity.

Think about it. World peace is actually an inside job. It starts with me and you. Little by little, positive change is possible and we can affect the whole.

Doing my inner work I know is rippling to all life, for the greater good. Everything that helped me heal and become me, I now share and offer at our Retreat Centre where it is my passion to assist women to rise and reclaim their lives beyond the effects of trauma.

In my last four years in Germany I also studied multiple disciplines in Psyhcho-Therapeutic Body Work and movement therapy. I have also practiced and studied Sound Healing, various modalities of Massage, Shamanism, Life Coaching, and I developed my own form of Therapeutic Dance, gleaning from all I had learned in the various disciplines I studied.

I was also touched deeply by many Middle Eastern and Eastern Philosophies and Religions too. Though I do not feel a strong connection to any organized religion, I see the beauty and truth that each offer in their own and unique ways. Love is Love no matter where you go.

I see the Oneness of the wisdoms that are often buried beneath the dogmas of man in each religion. If there was a path for me as a following, it would be Sufism for they embrace all life, all beliefs, all religions and people. As Rumi once said, "My religion is Love." As is mine.

Sharing some of my life story here in this book and practicing the healing work I do is my small way of upholding and feeding Love and being the change I want to see in the world.

As my writing mentor once said 'We are here to share our life stories with each other, if not why are we here. Through sharing we learn and we grow together."

GRATITUDES

I am so grateful, for everything, for every experience, every challenge, every joy I have lived. To be able to say that and really feel that after living through what I did is a phenomenal reality and accomplishment for me. I often send gratitude back to my past self that never gave up.

My life is more fulfilling and beautiful then I could ever have imagined it could be, including with its challenges at times. Life will always be life; full of paradox and duality where there are and always will be challenges, triggers, and pain at times for me to grow through. That's a given. I embrace it all. I still stumble at times, but I have the tools to get back up more swiftly now when I do.

Being Spiritual and a Healer does not mean I am perfect or that struggles, illness and challenges cease. That is a gross misconception many carry. Being Spiritual and a Healer just means that my capacity to be present, navigate and direct life experiences toward growth, love, and creativity is stronger.

I continue to meet myself, heal and grow whenever situations in life challenge me that brings me in touch with new spaces and places within me that need a touch of healing, shaping, and polishing. For me life is a constant journey of learning and refining. As long as we are alive we are students of life. There is always more to learn. I am grateful for that!

I am so grateful for all the Magic, Grace and Miracles my life has been blessed and upheld with. Magic is real. We just need to rise up to the highest good and truest expression of good in our heart, soul and lives to activate it.

As Paramahansa Yogananda once said, "We all have a super power to create our lives, but if we do not know how to use it we are stuck" It is true. I am so grateful to him and his courage to bring his teachings to the West in the 1920's.

Life has taught me that when we show up to the unlimited possibilities that abound in every moment with an open heart, when we take the risk and leap out beyond our comfort zone to follow our dreams and soul inspirations, magic happens!

Providence moves when we do, and opens unimaginable possibilities to us when we overcome our fears and we commit to our healing and becoming.

I am also so grateful to be married to the most amazing man I have ever known, who I can grow with, who meets me in every way, my soul mate, my best friend, my everything, who's love continually lifts me and my wings higher and higher. Through him I have a beautiful son who I love and adore beyond anything. They fill my heart with so much joy, there are no words.

I am grateful to have healed my relationships with my parents to the point there is now only love. The relationship with my sister is still a work in progress, but we are connecting more again now. Healing is happening.

I am grateful to Nature for teaching me to play the flute, I never took music lessons. The trees, mountains, rivers and streams taught me everything. My flute playing has led to producing two meditation CD's that are touching people's lives, Reunited: The Journey Home and Chakra Radiance. When I picked up my first bamboo flute I never could have imagined it could lead to this.

I am also extremely grateful to the most loving couple my husband and I know, Shera and Chidakash, who with their love made it possible that my husband and I now own and operate the most beautiful Retreat Centre on Galiano Island in BC, Serenity By The Sea, that they designed and built with so much love and where I now have the privilege of sharing my love of Nature and all I have learned and studied with my clients who come for personal healing retreats.

I get to experience beauty and magic every day. My words could never encompass the fullness of my heart and the depth of gratitude that dwells there. I am humbled every day by the greatness of Love, Life and God, the living Spirit of all life.

Here I am now. Wow! Writing this book brought a whole other layer of integration and healing to me in the process. It's been magical.

Now approaching 50 years of living I am still filled with childlike wonder and awe of life, even more so now actually. That is also a spectacular feat for me. There were times I felt I would never be able to reclaim that part of me and I missed that part of me so deeply for a long time. It is hard to live when we loose touch with our inner light and joy. I am grateful I fought my way through to feel it so fully again.

I am so Grateful to all of Nature, for all the incredible places my little feet have wondered and touched the Earth, all the beauty my eyes have seen. Nature, as a reflection of God, Christ, Buddha, Allah, Great Spirit, all the great Masters that have been on this Earth to guide us to a better way. These always will be my constant source of inner and outer guidance and orientation.

My gratitude goes also to all the incredible people I met along the way who gave me their time, insight, love, friendship and support. There are so many. My heart also extends gratitude for those who "harmed" me. They were important mirrors for me to know myself.

Kina Ole.

I genuinely hope that some of the magic of my journey and the wisdoms and insights that helped me have touched and inspired you in some way. That what I have shared here might open your heart and mind to connect to yourself and Nature more and that you can embrace the possibilities of healing and the love that are always there, the Spirit of Aloha, pulsing in every second, for you to connect to and use to create the life of your deepest joy and dreams.

Please know and always remember… you are stronger than you think you are and you are more capable and empowered than you can imagine. You also have more support then you realize.

You are not alone.
You belong.
You are enough.
You are important.
You are Loved.
Life/Love needs you.

This is the message I hope my book will ripple to you and the world.

There is a force of abundant good always available to you. We are made of the same stuff. The resilience and Love in Nature is in me, is in you, is in every living thing.

For me this is our deepest and most common thread; we are all Souls born from the same source of Love, lets connect there shall we? We are all intricately connected in this majestic web of life. We each have a story, we are also all fighting a battle inside, the very same battle, to belong and be enough. Please be kind to yourself and all living beings. We don't have to like everybody to simply be kind.

Yes we need boundaries, yes, we need to say no at times, yes we need to stand up for our rights to be treated right, but we do not need to do that with hate in our hearts to accomplish that.

We do have the power to change our world and the world around us, moment by moment, choice by choice, little by little.

Love Prevails all Trauma
E'Aloha E'

Blessings of Love, Light and Goodness to you all.

Manufactured by Amazon.ca
Bolton, ON

15740471R00150